Contemporary Film Directors

Edited by Justus Nieland and Jennifer Fay

The Contemporary Film Directors series provides concise, well-written introductions to directors from around the world and from every level of the film industry. Its chief aims are to broaden our awareness of important artists, to give serious critical attention to their work, and to illustrate the variety and vitality of contemporary cinema. Contributors to the series include an array of internationally respected critics and academics. Each volume contains an incisive critical commentary, an informative interview with the director, and a detailed filmography.

A list of books in the series appears at the end of this book.

Su Friedrich

Barbara Mennel

UNIVERSITY
OF
ILLINOIS
PRESS
URBANA,
CHICAGO,
AND
SPRINGFIELD

Frontispiece: Su Friedrich. Photo credit: Alexander Tuma. Image courtesy
of Su Friedrich

Names: Mennel, Barbara Caroline, author.
Title: Su Friedrich / Barbara Mennel.
Description: Urbana : University of Illinois Press, [2023] | Series: Contemporary
film directors | Includes bibliographical references, filmography, and index.
Identifiers: LCCN 2023000627 (print) | LCCN 2023000628 (ebook) | ISBN
9780252045288 (cloth) | ISBN 9780252087417 (paperback) | ISBN 9780252054808
(ebook)
Subjects: LCSH: Friedrich, Su. | Women motion picture producers and directors—
United States—Biography. | Lesbians in motion pictures.
Classification: LCC PN1998.3.F784 M46 2023 (print) | LCC PN1998.3.F784 (ebook) |
DDC 791.4302/33092—dc23/eng/20230330
LC record available at https://lccn.loc.gov/2023000627
LC ebook record available at https://lccn.loc.gov/2023000628

Contents

Acknowledgments |

First and foremost, I thank Su Friedrich. She accompanied the development of this project with the same exacting care that she extends to her films. Generous with her time for an extended interview, she also provided high-resolution images to accompany the text. Thank you to Donna Binder for sharing an image of the Lesbian Avengers demonstrating in the early 1990s.

I am grateful to Daniel Nasset, University of Illinois Press editor-in-chief, for his openness to ideas and ability to run with them. Also at the press, assistant acquisitions editor Mariah Mendes Schaefer was a reliable, fast, efficient, and kind interlocutor who took the time to talk to me on the phone about the book's production process.

During the writing process, invitations by Valerie Weinstein to discuss a section of the manuscript with the students in her graduate seminar Feminist Film Theory in Women's Studies at the University of Cincinnati and by Jaimey Fisher to present at the University of California Davis Humanities Institute were invaluable. Sabine Hake and Katrin Sieg are exceptional professional friends who brought their astute ability to identify threads in a developing text to an early draft. Kaira Cabañas and Amy Ongiri accompanied the process with support and understanding for what is at stake in writing a book.

This is a pandemic book. I wrote it primarily over two summers in different levels of lockdown. I could not have done it without the colleagues in the virtual humanities writing groups at the University of Florida in the summers of 2020 and 2021. The format of daily morning meetings anchored us in a rhythm that structured a world that had seemingly lost all of its moorings. The daily conversations about scholarly writing kept me on task and also reminded me to keep the call of administrative demands at bay. I also appreciated the attentive reading and textual engagement by the members of my virtual writing group of current and former PhD students: Faith Boyte, Lauren B. Cox, Felipe González-Silva, Claudia Hoffmann, Tyler Klatt, and Loren Pilcher.

The manuscript's two anonymous reviewers offered knowledgeable, insightful, and, in instances, challenging feedback. I thank them for the intellectual rigor of the engagement and the generosity of their time, as they provided additional references and paid attention to detail. Similarly, the series editors Justus Nieland and especially Jennifer Fay were encouraging, patient, and flexible, inviting creative readings.

I could not have done this without the support, encouragement, and trust in the project by Jeffrey S. Adler.

A Politics of the Personal in
Experimental Filmmaking

Auteurism Expanded

Independent filmmaker Su Friedrich fashioned a unique cinema out of
the influences of the avant-garde film movement in late 1970s New York
City. As an experimental director, she has forged a remarkable body
of work that blends features from structural film, such as an emphasis on abstract editing patterns, with political critique, for example,
exposing the way in which the medical industry dismisses women's
health concerns. Friedrich combines these different impulses into a
political and poetic oeuvre that invites simultaneous cinephilic and
activist responses. An active participant in the second-wave women's
movement, she made films that express its prominent slogan that the
personal is political (see Hanisch). Throughout her career, Friedrich
has participated in revolutionizing hierarchies through collectivizing
living and working contexts. Her cinema counters traditional heterosexuality by reorganizing ingrained narrative conventions and advocates

for lesbian-feminist aesthetics across different technological modes and historical periods. After four decades of filmmaking, she calls a filmography her own that radically reimagines cinema as an intensely personal art form. By infusing her films with her biography and exposing her emotions, anxieties, and health challenges, she engages in a unique form of public intimacy.

After primarily shooting, directing, and editing on 16 mm film throughout her early career, in the twenty-first century Friedrich tends to work in digital video. She foregrounds the materiality of her films and the diverse technologies of her filmmaking. Throughout the 1980s, for example, she scratched text into the celluloid of her black-and-white films, while in the twenty-first century she benefits from small cameras to shoot in doctors' offices. By the summer of 2022, Friedrich's body of work includes twenty-two titles, beginning with black-and-white silent 16 mm films, later 16 mm with sound, followed by color video with sound, and finally, in her most recent phase, digital video.[1] Their length ranges from one to eighty-one minutes. Her early experimental 16 mm films, from 1978 to 1982, fluctuate between six and sixteen minutes, and the majority are black-and-white. Especially the early films exhibit the grain structure of the medium. In addition, a time lag between shooting and projecting analog film results from the process that includes a developing bath, editing table, and optical printer, which infuses film with "eventfulness" (Youmans, "Performing" 126). This process is integral to the constitution of community in the act of collectively watching a film. After her early intermedial practice integrated performance art with film, Friedrich engages with the material effects of the digital turn in her later work. While she makes use of media-specific features, the defining characteristics of her filmmaking extend across the digital divide.

Friedrich's signature defines a coherent style. In her films, uniquely interwoven, different strands of diverse sources, predominantly footage that she shoots, but also recut archival material, inflect each other. She recontextualizes material from older feature films, integrates interviews, and on occasion also includes excerpts from home movies. Tactile practices shape Friedrich's cinema and foreground the materiality of objects through multiple strategies, including scratching of film and showing her hands in processes of embroidering, crafting, cutting, and drawing.

Her directorial presence and personal subjectivity mold her films into a cohesive oeuvre, with "profound connections" across the body of her work (Misra and Samer viii).

By focusing on Friedrich's work throughout her career, *Su Friedrich* attends to her signature across technological, social, and cultural transformations moving beyond the bifurcation between aesthetic and political categories. This book proposes an integrated analysis of formal cinematic experimentation and lesbian advocacy as a beginning and not an end point of analysis and opens up thematic considerations of gender, embodiment, memory, and temporality in analog and digital modes of documentary and experimental conventions. This volume advances several goals: to chart the significance of Friedrich as a director by providing an overview of her work; to foreground the characteristics that define her political-aesthetic signature; to situate her in the cultural, political, and historical contexts to which her work responds and which her films shape and which shape her films; and to expand the notion of auteurism so that it includes directors whose creative process occurs in communities that share political goals and engage in collaborations.

Su Friedrich proposes a concept of expanded auteurism. The figure of the auteur remains an ambivalent concept for women and minority directors. This is the case even though scholars have mobilized it for successful studies of individual feminist filmmakers (see, for example, Keller). An emphasis on the singular figure of the director defines cinephilic and scholarly discourses on experimental filmmaking more than for any other category, such as genre cinema or national film. The many volumes on members of the American avant-garde, for example, Hollis Frampton and Stan Brakhage, bespeak the way in which scholarship on auteurism shapes the discourse on a select few directors (on Frampton, see Moore; on Brakhage, see Baracco, James, Lori and Leslie, White, and Wodening; for a collection of Brakhage's interviews, see Ganguly). Publications by the directors themselves, their interviews, diaries, and reflections enable the filmmakers to shape public and scholarly discourse around their work (see, for example, Brakhage, *Essential, Film, Stan, Telling*; Frampton, *Circles, On the Camera*; for books, including published diaries, by Mekas, see Mekas, *Dance with Fred Astaire, I Had Nowhere to Go, Jonas Mekas, Movie Journal*, and *Words*). *Su Friedrich* asserts her significance for the history of experimental cinema while expanding its underlying notion of the auteur to be attentive to how gender and sexual politics shaped its formation in the first place and how feminist and lesbian filmmaking revised its practice and continue to do so.

From its inception, the term "auteur" provoked a debate whether it implied a masculine subject. In the late 1950s, members of the French New Wave employed the designation to advocate for art cinema while also delineating aesthetic signatures of Hollywood directors of the classic period. In 1957 French film critic André Bazin's concept of *la politique des auteurs* (the politics of the authors) emphasized personal artistic creation. Following this European lead, five years later, American film critic Andrew Sarris defined the distinctive quality of a filmmaker's oeuvre in the "recurring characteristic of style" as the author's "signature" (43). Critics alleged that the term implied elitist taste. In 1963 Pauline Kael, movie critic of the *New Yorker*, accused its advocates of celebrating personality instead of valuing aesthetic achievement. Comparing it to branding, she famously quipped: "It's like buying clothes by the label: this is Dior, so it's good" (50). Her rhetorical reference to high fashion contrasts starkly with the self-positioning of experimental filmmakers as outside of mainstream culture.

Friedrich's collaboratively engaged filmmaking practice fundamentally works against auteurism's ingrained notion of the singular director whose vision brings forth a film without accounting for informal and formal networks. Despite this masculinist tradition, scholars mobilized auteurism as a generative category for women and minority directors in the early twenty-first century. Film theorist Janet Staiger asserts the heightened significance of authorship for those who traditionally have been denied agency. The dearth of sole-author studies on women directors, in general, and experimental filmmakers, in particular, including Friedrich, demonstrates that scholars have not heeded Staiger's call. Auteurism's disavowal of historical, political, industrial, and communal contexts remains a stumbling block for an easy application to the works by directors who fuse politics with aesthetics.

Friedrich redefines the understanding of the artist by collaborating with experimental and lesbian filmmakers, artists, and painters. Frequent interlocutors include directors Peggy Ahwesh and Leslie Thornton, among others, as well as documentary filmmaker Janet Baus.

Friedrich also works with her partner, painter Cathy Nan Quinlan; writer Cynthia Carr; and dancer and filmmaker Yvonne Rainer. Other directors, such as Barbara Hammer, share several characteristic traits, for example, scratched text in the medium, an emphasis on tactility, and the recombinatory use of archival materials, particularly as it pertains to lesbian representation.

Expanded auteurism emphasizes the conditions of film production and circulation, as well as the commitment to social movements, critical traditions, and communities. The model validates mutual exchange that defines aesthetic and political programs in the face of film studies' lack of attention to collaborative film production (see Columpar 6). It serves alternative public spheres made up of strangers that form communities around shared texts. Lesbian experimental cinema fulfills such a function for queer subcultures.

Su Friedrich's open-ended and fluid sense of auteurism acknowledges the self-reflexive history of politically engaged filmmaking. Feminist directors who emerged out of the second-wave women's movement thematized collaboration on screen. For example, in her 1977 West German film *The All-Around Reduced Personality*, Helke Sander depicts a group of feminists who form a collective in order to apply for funding for a photography project about a female perspective on divided Berlin. The film captures the logistical, ideological, and interpersonal challenges of antihierarchical artistic labor. More-recent feminist practices include joint production companies (see Baer and Fenner). Minority directors founded the Sankofa Film and Video Collective and the Black TV and Film Collective to foreground solidarity in filmmaking and distribution practices. Migrant filmmakers, for example Turkish German award-winning director Fatih Akın, draw on their communities to create teams, including lay actors, who accompany them throughout their career.

This continuous expanded auteurism throughout Friedrich's career links alternative production forms to the current moment as collectivity has resurfaced in the twenty-first century. Feminist film collectives burst into prominence after 1968 internationally, from France to Canada, in search of utopian visions (on France, see Murray; on Canada, see Bociurkiw, esp. 6). Sharing the creative process not only organizes forms of production but also shapes filmic aesthetics and content. After a period of disenchantment with the idea of solidarity, collective practices are resurging in the twenty-first century to counter new labor conditions, precarity, the rise of neoliberalism, and the erosion of the public sphere (the *Camera Obscura* Collective, "Collectivity"; see also Ivanchikova, esp. 65).

Auteurism's customary focus on the singular creative subject contributed to the lack of attention to women filmmakers, in general, and led to a delayed recognition of female experimental directors, in particular. It took until the turn to the twenty-first century for film scholars to publish edited volumes on women in experimental cinema (see Blaetz; Petrolle and Wexman) and for collections on avant-garde cinema, documentary filmmaking, and new American cinema to include chapters on female filmmakers, including Friedrich (see Dixon and Foster; Gaines and Renov; Lewis). Important articles in these volumes situate Friedrich's filmmaking in the context of queer cinema (Holmlund, "Films"), social advocacy (Russell, "Culture"), and ethnography and domesticity (Renov, "New Subjectivities"). In those collections, scholars read her work's formal strategies closely (Wees) and relate them to political advocacy (Cutler).

Influential scholars of feminist and queer film, such as Chris Holmlund, William C. Wees, and Catherine Russell, forge arguments about Friedrich's oeuvre that move away from the singular-director model by pairing Friedrich with other feminist or queer filmmakers. Holmlund connects Friedrich with younger queer director Sadie Benning in one essay ("When Autobiography") and to Austrian avant-garde performance artist Valie Export in another ("Feminist"). Both Russell ("Culture") and Wees consider Friedrich in conjunction with her collaborators Ahwesh and Thornton, and Child and Thornton, respectively. These approaches highlight collaboration and comparison, sidestepping notions of singularity, which underwrites the traditional understanding of authorship. Yet, advancing solidarity in a society that celebrates individual achievement runs the danger of undermining efforts to validate the work of individual women directors, such as Friedrich.

Bolstering the concept of expanded auteurism, *Su Friedrich* embraces an understanding of biography and lived experience as human embeddedness in sociality, collectivity, and the body. This framework derives from Friedrich's filmography and the figure of the director as an embodied member of the lesbian feminist community. With her process of radically translating her own experience into experimental cinema, Friedrich represents a particularly important object of an auteur study with an oeuvre that challenges, probes, and investigates how subjects produce history and how history produces subjects.

The Politics of Biography

By exploring how Friedrich's life intimately shapes her films, this book presumes that biographies simultaneously belong to and exceed their historical contexts. Friedrich participated in social movements from feminism to lesbian activism and from antimilitarism to struggles against gentrification. In other words, her films not only insist on the particularity of lesbian history but also reflect how subcultural practices shape cultural imagination, especially that of New York City. Friedrich's continuous radical positionality creates an ongoing thread throughout her work, tightly interlacing of personal, political, and aesthetic concerns throughout her career.

Particularly, the combination of experimental aesthetics and lesbian politics makes the work productive for a new generation of political advocates, film aficionados, and cinema scholars. The films provide a record of the complexity of feminist, lesbian, and queer activism, in contrast to projections of cultural essentialism and mainstream identity politics onto these social movements of the late twentieth century. Academics have begun to revisit films by experimental lesbian filmmakers of that generation to question scholarship's common notion of a bifurcated distinction between performativity, associated with deconstructive queer theory, and essentialism, projected onto second-wave feminism and gay and lesbian liberation (Youmans, "Performing" 120). Building on important scholarship about Friedrich's experimental strategies and lesbian politics, *Su Friedrich* expands the interpretive frame to embrace questions of history and memory, aging and the body, and 16 mm and digital video, all of which she investigates through her personal-political perspective.

Friedrich consistently infuses films with her own experiences to propel lesbian feminist politics forward. As Ann Cvetkovich points out, for lesbian filmmakers of the period "intimate relationships are crucial to the public record and should not be cordoned off from the work" ("Artist" 39). Friedrich situates her own voice prominently but as part of a communal understanding of social subjects, including her family members. This deeply autobiographical thread—embedded in historical moments—connects her different films across their thematic diversity, aesthetic range, and stylistic choices. Repeatedly but not always, her voice-over narration defines her authorial signature. In other instances, however, multiple voices, narratives, and memories create a sense of a shared subjectivity that expresses lesbian desire, feminist consciousness, queer disruptions, class solidarity, and family relations. Friedrich's countercultural positions and political strategies organize how she blends documentary with experimental montage, ethnographic observation with activism, and narrative with interviews. She captures her own mundane everyday experiences, including minor affects, such as annoyance, and ugly emotions, such as rage. Those intimate vignettes reveal systemic structures of economic inequality and thus invoke a counterpublic.

Her directorship moves beyond the two dominant paradigms of political filmmaking: montage that emerged out of Bolshevik cinema, and social realism, a film language that feminist and left-wing filmmakers embraced in the 1970s and onward to document oppression. Thus, Friedrich rejects both the dialectic synthesis and the narrative resolution and, instead, calls upon spectators to experience her films viscerally and reflect on them intellectually. Her cinema addresses audience members' affective reactions and invites them to engage with the individual films with their cognitive, emotional, and linguistic abilities. Friedrich expresses the personal, and its attendant features, such as dreams and fantasies, in the formal experimental language of antirealist cinema with poetics, rhythm, and associative editing. The emphasis on subjectivity articulates collective experiences by those on the margins, including lesbians, girls, female patients, displaced working-class residents, and the elderly. This political commitment, both rooted in explicit lesbianism and exceeding its identity politics, defines her work and sets it apart.

Twentieth-century global events shaped Friedrich's family life. Her mother had grown up in Nazi Germany and emigrated to the United States after she met Friedrich's father, who had been stationed with the US military in Germany after World War II. Friedrich was born in New Haven, Connecticut, where her father was a professor at Yale University. She enjoyed an upbringing full of culture, from Greek mythology to classical and popular music, traces of which still germinate in her films. Her family reflects the educated middle class, in which a publicly liberal father advanced a stellar academic career after abandoning Friedrich's mother and siblings and remarrying twice. A prominent linguist and anthropologist, he later moved to the University of Chicago. Friedrich herself attended the University of Chicago (1971–1972) and Oberlin College (1972–1975), where she earned a bachelor of arts in art and art history with an emphasis on photography.

Friedrich's biographical trajectory belongs to the experience of a particular generation of women. Born in 1954 she is part of a cohort who came into political consciousness with second-wave feminism, participated in lesbian activism in the 1990s, and subsequently confronted twenty-first-century neoliberal capitalism. As a result, she experienced the invigorating and exuberating opening of institutions to women while informal networks of male friendships persisted in determining status and access. This was also the case in the circles of the New York City avant-garde, which included women but continued old habits of viewing them as muses and stars. At the same time, filmmaking enabled these cinefeminists to expose the gendered power dynamics pervasive in and beyond the film world.

Friedrich's generation of feminists redefined the public sphere, advancing what the slogan "The personal is political" captures. Yet, many members of that cohort now find themselves increasingly marginalized as they become older, their lasting political influence and artistic importance notwithstanding. Women do not accrue value with increasing years in a society obsessed with the image. In addition, the movement to catapult the personal into the limelight emerged from a society in which the private was distinct, feminized, and lesser-valued than the public sphere. As politics and technology erode privacy, the Right appropriates the discourse of personal choice, and visual and social media culture permeates the public with curated selves for consumption, the claim that the personal is political loses its catalyzing force. These processes appropriate and undermine the advances by second-wave feminists.

Friedrich's intervention into the avant-garde occurred in the context of the postwar history of American experimental cinema. Throughout the 1940s and 1950s, the films of this movement—alternately labeled avant-garde, experimental, underground, and independent—privileged the personal in a radical aesthetic divergence from the chronological, cause-effect logic of continuity editing of mainstream cinema, particularly Hollywood. European art cinema of the 1950s and 1960s, including its distribution system in art-film houses and expanding markets in the United States, motivated American directors to establish a counter cinema to mainstream Hollywood and television.

In this process, the American avant-garde cinema simultaneously included and marginalized women experimental filmmakers. Sidelined artists include Shirley Clarke, Marie Menken, Carolee Schneemann, Storm De Hirsch, Barbara Rubin, and Yoko Ono. Feminist film scholar Patricia Mellencamp provocatively asserts that experimental cinema outdid its mainstream counterpart in its misogyny, arguing that women were actually "worse off in Soho or San Francisco than in Hollywood" because, according to her, the homoerotic work by experimental filmmakers Jean Cocteau, Jack Smith, and Kenneth Anger linked pleasure and femininity to death (22). Her stunning accusation about the experimental avant-garde reflects a perspective that presumes an absolute dividing line between feminism and queer politics, a boundary that was more prevalent in 1990 than in the following years.

Friedrich's Oeuvre

When Friedrich arrived in New York City in 1976, she found both experimental film and the second women's movement well underway. The emerging director developed her signature style with six short experimental films in the brief period between 1978 and 1982. During these early years of her career, Friedrich primarily shot silent films on 16 mm, except for her first short film, *Hot Water* (1978), for which she blew up Super 8 mm to 16 mm for a sound film. She varied length between six and sixteen minutes and generally used black-and-white film stock and shot on a "16mm silent Bolex" (Misra and Samer ix). Especially the four early films *Cool Hands, Warm Heart* (1979), *Scar Tissue* (1979), *Gently Down the Stream* (1981), and *But No One* (1982) encapsulate a distinct experimental aesthetics. She shot footage in streets and sport centers, at swimming pools, and on the beach. Her emphasis on rhythm captures movement and stasis, contrast and similarity, repetition and variation. Scratched subjective poetics, haptic imaginary, and the performance of gender characterize her early films as part of an engagement with different art forms and media.

Representative of lesbian feminism of the second women's movement, Friedrich advanced a political avant-garde aesthetics that embodied key concepts of gender performance and lesbian desire that feminist film studies first and queer and transgender studies later theorized. My analysis of Friedrich's first set of films emphasizes the role that cinema plays in capturing cultural and social dynamics, which theory subsequently codifies. Her early experimental black-and-white films at the turn from the late 1970s to the early 1980s employ editing to subvert the dominant notion of binary gender, a political-aesthetic process that expresses feminist and lesbian politics and also invites readings informed by queer and transgender theoretical paradigms and activist claims. This book, therefore, employs the terms "women" and "men," "lesbian" and "gay," "queer," and "transgender" as distinct, overlapping, and adjacent categories. Contrary to presentist perceptions, before the emergence of queer activism and theory, gay and lesbian were "unruly, flexible, and capacious terms" that often included a range of political positions and nonnormative genders and sexual practices (Youmans, "Thank You" 11).

This volume argues for the centrality of feminist experimental cinema, in particular, Friedrich's complex integration of politics and experimental aesthetics for such a process of reassessment. *Su Friedrich* contributes to the "archival project" that studies the women's movement, especially its media cultures (Samer 29). Feminists seized the notion of lesbianism in their activism, scholarship, and creative and cultural work to reimagine gender and sexual existence (Samer 1). Scholar Rox Samer reconsiders 1970s lesbian feminism by studying "lesbian potentiality," which takes the "work of cultural feminism seriously" (6). These recent approaches are both indebted to queer theory but also counter its "rejection of the possibility of women's and gay liberation thinking in concert with queerness" (8). Samer shows that feminist historiography also does not need to ignore trans existence, because trans people partook in the "imagination that lesbian existence in the 1970s made possible" (34). Similarly, Clara Bradbury-Rance points out that although "lesbian" and "queer" neither fulfil their political potential equally nor advance the same theoretical function, they are both productive interrelated terms, as "queer" includes the potential to move beyond the norms of difference and "lesbian" marks specific forms of marginality (14).

Lesbians played a key role in feminist experimentation in the late 1970s and 1980s, from American director Hammer to her West German counterparts Monika Treut and Ulrike Ottinger. Both a local and global development, 1970s cinefeminists from around the world engaged with film, video, and other visual moving arts to explore female subjectivity and to liberate the representation of women from the male gaze. Friedrich contributed to an international wave of women directors who innovated narratives and aesthetics while she mined the energy and infrastructure of avant-garde New York City. Those independent women filmmakers advanced cinefeminism before the emergence of New Queer Cinema in the early 1990s, including, for example, Rainer and Hammer, who began working in experimental film before Friedrich, Ahwesh, and Thornton. These diverse filmmakers provided a context in which Friedrich made films, audiences watched them, and critics reviewed them. A case in point, Hammer shared with Friedrich an original interest in photography and painting before turning to experimental cinema. Yet, Hammer's work also differs as it foregrounds lesbian sexuality, particularly, in *Nitrate Kisses* (1992) and *History Lessons* (2000). This cohort participated in dedicated film festivals, for example, on experimental queer cinema, where they engaged with each other in conversations about form and content, reflecting on their art practice with each other in the public sphere and asserting visual expression of lesbian subjectivity and authorship.

During the 1980s a group of feminist filmmakers exploded onto the film scene with personal and political films. These female directors highlighted subjectivity in oppositional discourses to define a counterculture (Petrolle and Wexman 2). In addition to Ahwesh, Hammer, Rainer, and Thornton, they included Abigail Child, Jill Godmilow, and Lynne Sachs, among others. Tethering experimental strategies with observational ethnographies, biography with social documentary, and feminism with lesbian politics, these directors continued the aesthetics of experimental cinema and often collaborated on or supported each other's projects.

In that period, Friedrich created intimate films about memory and family, such as *The Ties That Bind* (1984) and *Sink or Swim* (1990). These longer, sound films weave her biography into the experimental film language by questioning her mother about Nazi Germany and confronting her absent father. Mobilizing different documentary modes, they explore her own memories in relation to her parents. They challenge the patriarchal organization of the nuclear family and its constitutive silences that undergird its bourgeois formation. These personal films that foreground subjective familial memories bookend a third film, *Damned If You Don't* (1987), which integrates collective remembrances with the rewriting of a mainstream midcentury film and a lesbian love story. Subjective memory defines Friedrich's three films throughout the decade of the 1980s.

Marking a generational shift, in May 1989 a rift opened among avant-garde directors when a new cohort asserted itself. Primarily women and gay experimental filmmakers signed a public letter of protest challenging the official history of the International Experimental Film Congress, which was to be held that spring in Toronto, and denouncing the institutionalized canon of purported masterworks (see Ahwesh et al.,). Signatories included Friedrich, Ahwesh, Child, Hammer, Rainer, and Thornton, queer filmmakers Todd Haynes and Tom Kalin, and producer Christine Vachon. The letter objected to the exclusion of new work and the fact that directors could participate only if they paid $100 for their work to be screened. The document accused the organizers of limiting projection in the official program to representatives of the already established generation that was holding on to its power. The authors and signatories concluded by announcing themselves as the rightful heirs to the aesthetic and political program: "The Avant-Garde is dead; long live the avant-garde" (Ahwesh et al., 101). The gesture of a public letter proclaimed a collective identity, exposed the self-anointed artistic leadership, and decried the fossilization of the former cutting-edge understanding of the art form. The letter writers demanded their place in a generational succession.

From this moment of self-assertion, throughout the 1990s, Friedrich directs political films that explicitly center on lesbian experiences, desires, and activism. Her titles confront discrimination, document direct action, meditate on a breakup, and explore collective memories of lesbian childhood. During the decade of the 1990s, she blossoms into an activist, incorporates the documentary form into her films, and participates in collaborative projects foregrounding lesbian identity. The films *First Comes Love* (1991), *Lesbian Avengers Eat Fire, Too*

(1993), *Rules of the Road* (1993), and *Hide and Seek* (1996) mobilize a collective identity.[2] For lesbians, asserting the everyday, in the form of remembering childhood or experiencing lost love, constitutes a political act. With her films, Friedrich participated in the 1990s culture wars by claiming same-sex desire in the public sphere. She joined the Lesbian Avengers, an activist group founded in 1992 with chapters in fifty-five cities. In addition, by regularly accompanying screenings of her films at university campuses and film festivals, she extended the personal dimension beyond the film texts into the public sphere.

The emergence of New Queer Cinema in the early 1990s had a paradoxical effect on the reception of her films (Rich, "New"). It provided Friedrich with an expanded audience and increased critical attention to her work, but it also cast her as a precursor to queer films made by young directors who appeared at the film festival circuit. When "queer" became the umbrella term for the range of sexualities and genders, its activism and theory sidelined the explicit critique of institutional heteronormativity and masculinist chauvinism of the previous years.

The politicization of private life led Friedrich to alternative lifestyles from those of her parents' generation. Beginning in 1989, she lived in a loft in a former factory in Williamsburg, Brooklyn, New York, with Quinlan and other artists. Their living space included a studio and a place to screen films. As Friedrich documents eloquently in her film *Gut Renovation* (2012), neoliberal economies created rampant gentrification, forcing her and her partner to leave the upscaled neighborhood.[3]

Delving into sickness, aging, and gentrification in a diaristic mode, Friedrich continues in the twenty-first century to explore the political aspect of her personal life. The themes reflect the biographical dimension of her and her family's aging process and the changing political circumstances as neoliberal capitalism usurps niche spaces of alternative social and economic structures through aggressive urban displacements. Her films turn to the discarded and the displaced, whom society considers irrelevant. Friedrich's twenty-first-century titles are digital video in color and with sound except for her sixty-five-minute *The Odds of Recovery* (2002), which she shot primarily on 16 mm film. Her self-reflective video *Seeing Red* (2005) makes use of the immediate feedback loop.

Friedrich's current film practice takes place in the visually oversaturated world of social media and streaming platforms. The changed relationships of producers and consumers, makers and audiences have reconfigured the constellation of private and public, which differs from the moment when feminists coined the motto that the personal is political. Her film *I Cannot Tell You How I Feel* (2016) about the move of her mother from Chicago to New York City shares the documentation of the everyday with the all-pervasive diaristic mode of visual self-representation and documentation. Yet, in contrast to the endless proliferation of self-referential short videos that circulate globally, Friedrich's digital videos critically investigate her own subjectivity and continue her lifelong engagement with memory. In a world that fetishizes the immediacy of the glitzy, new, and young, her work carefully explores the effects of aging on memory and the body, in regard to her mother and herself. *I Cannot Tell You How I Feel* includes images from Friedrich's 1984 *The Ties That Bind* about her relationship to her mother, thereby invoking not only the passing of biological time but also highlighting the continuity of her filmmaking. The inclusion of Friedrich's earlier film highlights her role as a director of an extensive oeuvre.

The Poetics of Titles

Friedrich's film titles encapsulate the experimental quality of her cinema. Their enigma consistently evokes curiosity but also confers meaning into the viewing process. They intrigue and interpellate spectators into an active engagement by rejecting obvious denotations about the films' contents. They complicate consumption. Repeatedly, Friedrich achieves this effect by using fragments of figures of speech or ambivalent references for her titles. She describes them as "play with some known expression or adage or part of a song" (Martin 69). For example, *The Ties That Bind*, about her mother's memories of Germany and Friedrich's connection to her mother, conjures up abstract and metaphorical meanings. That way, the titles link the films' autobiographical discourse to a larger context and point beyond the person of Friedrich. The phrase "ties that bind" evokes the blood bonds among family members that tether individuals to their kinship, nation, and history. Yet, literal ties that bind also capture limitations and restrictions. Belonging to a national history, such as the Nazi period in Germany, creates a wrought relationship to one's past, which extends to the next generation. While the title captures this central ambivalence of belonging to one's family and its legacy, the multiple meanings only unlock retroactively after viewing the film.

In other instances, film titles reverse the common understanding of familiar phrases. *Damned If You Don't* evokes a saying as the second part of "damned if you do, damned if you don't." The title triggers the audience's association by providing a fragment that implies a prior whole. The complete phrase suggests two paths forward, but no matter the action one undertakes, it will be futile. What appears as choice might not be one at all. Omitting the first half of this two-part saying changes the connotation but also leaves it open and ambivalent. Again, only the viewing process unlocks the significance of the title. As the film explores desire and religion, "damned if you don't" assumes additional literal meaning. Whereas Christianity codifies behaviors by outlining prohibitions, such as not to covet thy neighbor's wife, in the context of the film's endorsement of lesbian love, the title becomes a clarion call to act on desire. Similarly, *Sink or Swim* continues Friedrich's convention of employing an enigmatic phrase, the significance of which the film reveals over the course of several of its narrative vignettes. While the saying "sink or swim" references the need to engage in immediate action in order to survive, its literal meaning horrifically evokes danger and interpellates a subject into self-reliance in isolation and without support. The title refers to Friedrich's father's attitudes toward her as a child, when, in an anecdote in the film, he throws her in the pool. The isolated phrase makes visible the inherent violence in normalized pedagogy. *Sink or Swim* as a title announces Friedrich's method of exposing the cruelty inherent in conventional social relations that patriarchal parenting produces.

Friedrich's film titles are an integral part of her method of critiquing existing norms and invoking innovative forms of love, life, and art. In instances, they address those familiar with subcultural references as part of a shared discourse community. Participants of queer culture in the 1990s would recognize the name Lesbian Avengers and be familiar with their activity of eating fire. Yet, again, the title evokes a question that unsettles its meaning. What does "too" modify? Does it imply others who eat fire, such as magicians and circus performers, or does it refer to the group's many activities? Titles that create ambivalence and provoke questions invite audience members to be active viewers and reflexive participants in the meaning-making of a film.

In other instances, titles are indirectly related, such that they ask viewers to reflect on the connection to the film's concern. *Rules of the Road*, for instance, does not reveal that this is a film about a breakup, instead ironically invoking the orderly flow of traffic. While much of the footage depicts cars on city streets, the film examines the emotional afterlife of lost love. Traffic rules are red herrings, displaced symbols for an emotional story that comments on cinema's ability to obscure as much as it reveals. The repeated images of station wagons in New York City provide a visual language for a narrative about the state of a breakup.

Scar Tissue is similarly one of the more enigmatic titles of Friedrich's films. There is no literal or sematic direct relation between the title and the men and women walking or what the larger context of the images invoke. In other words, we neither see scars nor tissue nor accidents. Instead, the film generates questions: Does *Scar Tissue* refer to Friedrich's filmmaking, the scratching of celluloid and the cutting of film? Does it extend the haptic dimension of her film into a metaphor of film itself, as that which grows together in a new way after the cut?

Hide and Seek, as a children's game titling a film about lesbian girlhood, has a metonymic relationship to its content. A familiar game can stand in for childhood in a way that traffic does not represent lesbian love. By employing a metonymic title, Friedrich implies a relationship to filmic content that moves beyond documentary truth. This title invites literal and metaphoric readings. In the play, some hide, and one seeks. Do the adult interviewees who reflect on their lesbian youth seek out what was hidden from themselves? Does film as a medium reveal what the world concealed from the girls? The titles generate questions and extend the engagement beyond the viewing of the individual films.

Four Clusters

This volume defines Friedrich's signature in four clusters of her films that analyze the progression of her oeuvre's style. Out of the twenty-two films that she has made over her career, fifteen feature prominently in this book. This leaves aside primarily films that appeared either in the early or late period of her filmmaking when she developed her style in short films or created more and shorter digital films. Friedrich established herself as experimental filmmaker with her signature practice of scratching and rhythmic editing. She developed a film language that traces the process of gendering subjects, while eschewing normative narrative expectations. The next section, "Scratching and Cutting," engages her black-and-white silent films that she made in three years, *Cool Hands, Warm Heart* (1979), *Scar Tissue* (1979), *Gently Down the Stream* (1981), and *But No One* (1982), except for two short films, *Hot Water* (1978, 12 minutes), available on Vimeo, and *I Suggest Mine* (1980, 6 minutes), in Friedrich's private collection.

Throughout the 1980s, Friedrich increasingly engages familial and cultural remembrances, reflecting the processes of memory with films that become longer and include sound. The next section, "Counter Memories," maps out the filmic aesthetics that capture biography, desire, and memory in the context of politics and culture. The three titles *The Ties that Bind* (1984), *Damned If You Don't* (1987), and *Sink or Swim* (1990), made three years apart, define her work in the decade.

Lesbian and feminist politics become more forceful and explicit during the 1990s, accompanying queer activism in the so-called culture wars. While Friedrich's films in the decade mobilize different genres, they all advance lesbian visibility. "The Politics of Being Lesbian," the following section, covers the range her films made in the decade associated with the emergence of New Queer Cinema: *First Comes Love* (1991), *Lesbian Avengers Eat Fire, Too* (1993), *Rules of the Road* (1993), and *Hide and Seek* (1996).

In the twenty-first century, individual and collective precarious living conditions, such as aging and gentrification, circumscribe Friedrich's experience as part of a changed political landscape and thus make up the themes of her films, which participate in the digital turn. The final section, "Digital Embodiments" covers her important films of the period. *The Odds of Recovery* (2002), *Seeing Red* (2005), *Gut Renovation* (2012), and *I Cannot Tell You How I Feel* (2016) use documentary aesthetics in intimate self-reflexive and critically observational style. Friedrich continues her experimental-film language to make deeply political films that repeatedly capture the passing of time.

Focusing on those four substantive films, the final section leaves aside two short films, *The Head of a Pin* (2004, 21 minutes) and *Queen Takes Pawn* (2013, 6.5 minutes), part of her later more intimate, digital repertoire, even though these two films are available for viewers on the Su Friedrich DVD collection. In addition, in the twenty-first century

Friedrich made some films for hire, such as *From the Ground Up* (2008, 54 minutes), and *Practice Makes Perfect* (2012, 11 minutes), or as part of a collective project, for example *5/10/20* (2020, 2 minutes). The final section accords similar theoretical, aesthetic, artistic, philosophical, and political weight to those films as the scholarly discourse has given to her earlier experimental cinema, leaving aside the analysis of some films that would be redundant to the overarching argument. In short, this volume privileges in-depth discussion of the majority of Friedrich's oeuvre, including textual and contextual analyses of those films that advanced her career, claiming a comprehensive account of her authorship. Her oeuvre and its overarching stylistic characteristics enable Friedrich's exemplary significance across activism and art to come to the fore.

Scratching and Cutting

Friedrich's early films, made in the span of four years, develop an experimental film language that captures the construction of binary gender and offers alternative visions of women's sexuality. They emphasize formal composition, enigmatic poetics, and associative links between texts and images. Through the viewing process, the concern with women, gender, lesbian sexuality, labor, fantasy, and desire comes to the fore. These early works establish Friedrich's authorial signature in a recognizable style that emphasizes the rhythmic patterns of editing. Her unique use of texts, which she often scratches into the celluloid, endows her films with a haptic quality.

Between 1978 and 1982 Friedrich establishes herself as an avant-garde director with a cluster of black-and-white films that define her authorial signature of formal and thematic characteristics, including editing as a tool for rhythmic patterning. These films subtly express feminist politics and lesbian desire. The series of short 16 mm black-and-white experimental films *Cool Hands, Warm Heart* (1979), *Scar Tissue* (1979), *Gently Down the Stream* (1981), and *But No One* (1982) intercut images of gendered bodies and subjective fantasies. The films perform feminism through the language of experimental cinema, especially scratching and cutting of celluloid. In doing so, they expose how dominant notions of the public, history, and temporality traditionally rely on gender's imbrication with heterosexual desire. This cluster of films, I argue, sets the foundation for her oeuvre, which advances alternatives to hegemonic perspectives.

Friedrich's early work employs cinematic strategies to lay bare the ways in which repeated gestures construct gender in a binary system. Her films of the late 1970s and early 1980s emphasize the performativity of sex and gender. The cluster includes women engaged in female grooming in the form of performance art in the public, men and women moving working in the city, and Friedrich's dreamscapes.

Feminist art and experimental cinema, two artistic movements in the late 1970s, shape her early work. Combining cutting-edge practices of performance art and montage editing, the early films reveal the social construction of gender through accoutrements and generative enactments. A decade before the publication of Judith Butler's groundbreaking theory of gender performativity in her foundational work of queer studies, *Gender Trouble: Feminism and the Subversion of Identity* (1990), Friedrich's early films emphasize how repetitive gestures interpellate subjects into appearing feminine. Formal aesthetics organize the focus on gender, as the films intercut images in visual and temporal patterns through pacing, rhyming, and contrasting. Using repetition and variation, the films deconstruct gender's assumed natural existence. Contrasting shots expose the gendered production of bodies. Her films simultaneously resist traditional representation of femininity and demonstrate how normative gender intertwines with heterosexual desire. The feminist slogan that the personal is political motivates such a double move (see Hanisch). The films participate in the creation of a feminist and lesbian counterpublic while their diegesis also represents a public sphere.

Furthermore, Friedrich's oeuvre relies on a commitment to collective work, beginning in the late 1970s and continuing to the early twenty-first century. When in 2016, *Camera Obscura*, the preeminent feminist film-studies journal, dedicated two special volumes to the theory and practice of collectivity, several of the essays examined the feminist film collectives of the late 1970s and 1980s, while other articles took up networks as reemerging forms of community in the twenty-first century. Post-1968 radical politics envisioned collaboration, and technologies enabled it. Yet, interpersonal dynamics and conflicts in groups, political mainstreaming of feminist filmmaking, and economic tensions in cooperative projects led women to abandon these alternative models of organizing artistic labor. Questions that have animated collective practices have reemerged in the twenty-first century in the face of changing formations of private and public. Social movements, such as #MeToo, #BlackLivesMatter, and @changethemuseum, inflect political culture and confront art institutions anew, often mobilizing from digital platforms. They expose dynamics of discrimination and demand a reckoning with past and current practices to engender equity and inclusion. Friedrich's films speak to these concerns with a subtle and forceful foresight.

The four early films thematize the body in the public sphere in ways that feminist, queer, and transgender studies of materiality and identity later theorize. Beginning with *Cool Hands, Warm Heart*, Friedrich's oeuvre centrally stages the body in its gendered social formation, a theme that she continues throughout her career. These four films uniquely deconstruct femininity through performance. Transcending academic fields and political movements, from second-wave feminism to queer theory and transgender studies, these films focus on the body as a site to negotiate gender and sexuality (see Halberstam, *Masculinity*; Salamon). Such terms as "real" and "constructed" or "biological" and "cultural" encapsulate the shorthand for ongoing and shifting debates. Friedrich's artistic work thus not only provides a historical genealogy of key concepts of collectivity, the body, and the public but, more important, also contributes to the theoretical debate about paradigms of embodiment in feminist, queer, and transgender studies. Remaining steadfast throughout her career, Friedrich deconstructs the notion of the natural body through fragmentation, repetition, and performance while insisting on its materiality, including health, sexuality, and aging.

The twin engagement with experimental cinema and feminist collective labor defined Friedrich from the moment she arrived in New York City, the epicenter of feminist activism and experimental cinema, and discovered her love for film. She participated in the city's Millennium Film Workshop and in the collective *Heresies: A Feminist Publication on Art and Politics*. Such local institutions and organizations established a foundation for her feminist experimental film art. After previous training in photography at Oberlin College, she became fascinated by film's possibility of movement. The Millennium Film Workshop enabled affordable access to equipment and nonhierarchical teaching in informal settings where Friedrich participated in a three-night Super 8 mm workshop with David Lee.[4] By that time, the nonprofit media-arts center had existed for a decade as part of the federal government's antipoverty program. Under the tutelage of its first director, experimental filmmaker Ken Jacobs, the Millennium Film Workshop offered classes in cinematography, sound, and editing. Its five programs—the Personal Cinema Series, the Workshop Program, Equipment Access Service, the *Millennium Film Journal*, and the Millennium Gallery—sustained a comprehensive infrastructure for filmmakers from production to screening and film criticism. When Friedrich showed her early works in the Personal Cinema Series, she joined the ranks of experimental filmmakers who comprised the American avant-garde.

At the Millennium, Friedrich received an education outside of the traditional film school. She rented a camera for a dollar a day and used editing rooms for a monthly membership fee, which appeared to her as if "it cost nothing." Learning in informal ways from other filmmakers, foremost from Lee, introduced her to collaborative filmmaking. The Millennium provided access to screening rooms, editing facilities, and production equipment. Over the years, international luminaries, such as Jean-Luc Godard, Jim Jarmusch, Susan Seidelman, Oliver Stone, and Andy Warhol, used those resources. Later, Friedrich herself became an instructor at the Millennium. Filmmakers, critics, and scholars discussed theoretical, political, and practical aspects of experimental cinema in the *Millennium Film Journal*. The magazine carried the first critical article on Friedrich's films in 1983, which remained the sole scholarly publication on her work for a decade until the emergence of queer film theory in the early 1990s (Hanlon; on queer film theory, see Gever, Greyson, and Parmar; Rich, "New"; Bad Object Choices).

As part of the generation of second-wave feminists, Friedrich benefited from screenings at the Millennium Film Workshop and the Collective for Living Cinema, an artist-run cooperative in Lower Manhattan specializing in historical and contemporary avant-garde films. Eager to confront patriarchy, women became directors (see Cutler). Yet, institutional structures also sustained the unspoken support for advancing men at the expense of women. If female filmmakers pointed out their discrimination, developed a feminist profile, and advocated for lesbian issues, male directors accused them of overdetermining their art with politics. For women filmmakers, this dialectic dynamic of inclusion and exclusion permeated the culture of 1970s New York City avant-garde art and experimental cinema. The accessible and oftentimes public infrastructure enabled women to become filmmakers, while the cult of personality of individual filmmakers and the existing networks of friendship and admiration cemented male bonding and privileged individual men to rise to prominence.

Friedrich and other feminist and lesbian filmmaking colleagues encountered this ambivalent situation in the late 1970s and throughout the 1980s in New York City. On the one hand, the publicly funded institutions, such as the Millennium, embraced their presence and enabled their work. On the other hand, the social network of vanguard artists, blind to their own dynamics of exclusion, advanced fantasies of neutral objectivity. Peter Sempel, for example, remembers that Hammer was critical of Mekas because he ignored gay and lesbian filmmakers, to which Mekas answered that most gay and lesbian directors are "stressing too much their sex and society situation, although by now they should be 'normals between normals' and concentrate more on the possibilities of films 'normally'" (95).

Not only avant-garde filmmakers but also scholars were divided over new impulses. Friedrich's commitment to experimental cinema and feminist activism after her arrival in New York City occurred just as scholars developed theoretical paradigms of either mythical experimental cinema or feminist theory that diverged in contrasting trajectories of the two fields. Her work did not fit neatly into either camp of the binary. In 1974 American critic and scholar P. Adams Sitney published his defining book on myth and experimental cinema, *Visionary Film: The American Avant-Garde, 1943–2000*. The following year, film scholar Laura Mulvey penned her groundbreaking essay "Visual Pleasure and Narrative Cinema," which would shape feminist film studies for decades to come. Continuing her lead, academics privileged scholarship on Hollywood film, particularly the melodrama, to counter its previous abject status as the woman's film. Feminist film scholars also perceived Sitney's argument about the value of experimental cinema as a lightning rod. According to Mellencamp, his "sectarian disquisition" that scholars "repudiated or upheld" haunted the debate about avant-garde film (17).

Friedrich's work neither adhered to Sitney's model nor to feminist film theory's concern with classic narrative and a psychoanalytic approach to spectatorship.

Instead, Friedrich's 16 mm, sixteen-minute *Cool Hands, Warm Heart* conjoins feminist performance art and experimental cinema in its deconstruction of gender (figure 1). The performers, Donna Allegra Simms, Sally Eckhoff, Jennifer MacDonald, Rose Maurer, and Marty Pottenger are public-facing artists and not professional film actors. Playwright and performance artist Pottenger, for example, collaborated with working-class communities and unions. Such "alternative models of affective labor" distinguished experimental cinema from Hollywood's industrial mode of production (Osterweil 15). Taking its cues from feminist art activism, this early film captures multiple performances in a cinema verité environment of Orchard Street, a busy New York City location with a rich evocative history of immigration, experimental cinema, and arts movements. In a minimalist narrative, two women enjoy everyday

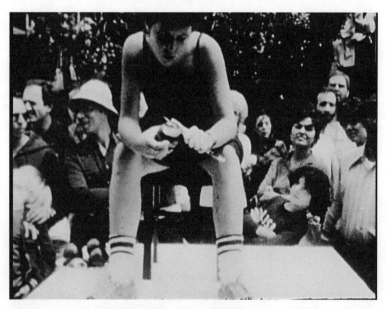

Figure 1. Performance in Orchard Street
in *Cool Hands, Warm Heart* (1979)

pleasures in the urban environment without exposition or a psychological motivation for the characters or action. Lacking an establishing shot, the film begins with a medium long shot traveling up the body of a young woman. She leans self-confidently against the wall of a building in a posture evocative of James Dean's iconic pose and gazes directly at the camera and, by extension, the audience. After several cuts, the camera focuses on another woman sitting on a chair on a pedestal amidst active foot traffic. She ritualistically rolls up her trousers and begins carefully and meditatively shaving her legs. Shoppers surround her with curiosity. The young woman from the opening shot approaches one of the performers and without speaking smears shaving cream on the sitting woman's legs and face. She then disappears into the crowd. Words scratched into celluloid spell out alliterations that add an intriguing, yet enigmatic, poetic text that does not explicate the images or the action.

As the first woman moves through the crowd and engages with the performances, she mediates the experience of looking and interacting for the audience. The film includes several rituals of female self-fashioning. A long shot captures Donna Allegra Simms in a solid stance on a pedestal before she crouches with a low-angle shot framing her in front of tenement houses (figure 2). Reclining on a chair, she cuts holes into her white sweater at her arm pits to shave her underarm hair. A crush of shoppers surrounds her to observe the spectacle. The first woman approaches a small mirror at a store selling sunglasses and applies eyeliner. The film shifts to another woman sitting atop a pedestal and braiding her long hair, when the woman moving through the crowd approaches her with a pair of scissors to cut her braid. In the final installment, the first woman sits on a table peeling apples. On a grainy background and with an erratic and jumpy effect appears a poetic text consisting of one word per image. The mobile female stranger pulls another woman off a table and takes her by her hand to dash to an arcade. The film transitions effortlessly from evoking high-art practice to the two women frolicking in the pop-cultural setting. There, dynamic camera movement captures the women playing a pinball machine and participating in a virtual car race. In the final sequence, they return on a bicycle to the now-empty streets.

Friedrich's commitment to feminist art, particularly performance art, and collaboration among women defines *Cool Hands, Warm Heart*.

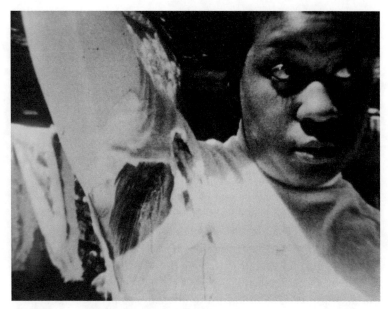

Figure 2. Donna Allegra Simms in
Cool Hands, Warm Heart (1979).
Image courtesy of Su Friedrich

It also bears witness to intertwined feminism and lesbian activism, which alternated between being intimately tethered to each other and being engaged in battles of differentiation. The collaboration among the women on screen reflects Friedrich's off-screen feminist embrace of collective work as an antihierarchical and antiauthoritarian form of organization. In 1977 Friedrich joined the women's collective that produced the magazine *Heresies*, published until 1993. She coedited its special volume "Lesbian Art and Artists" in fall 1977, to which she also contributed photographs (Carr et al., n.p.). *Heresies* forcefully commented on politics and gender in the art world. Working at the journal, Friedrich put her design, production, and office-management skills to use. Such alternative structures reflected the feminist understanding of the personal as political. Shared labor decentered the notion of the singular artist-creator in philosophical and material terms.

Cool Hands, Warm Heart captures the immediacy of performance art, including its corporeality and haptic quality and, thus, both validates and archives it despite its ephemerality. By cinematically documenting and, thus, arresting the fleeting encounters that emerge in the moment of live acts, Friedrich mediates performance art in a film through a process, which Jay David Bolter and Richard Grusin call "remediation." Feminism of the 1970s privileged performance art because it moved the body out of the private realm into public representation, a process it shared with the history of experimental cinema.

Friedrich's emphasis on the body in this 1979 film partook in experimental cinema's rejection of 1940s and early 1950s film culture. In the late 1950s American experimental cinema began investigating corporeality, addressing spectators as embodied participants, and replacing the symbolic language of the psychological cinema of the 1940s (Osterweil 12–13). While experimental cinema mobilized the body as "a site of ideological resistance," feminists were suspicious of claims to its inherent revolutionary ability in the public sphere (Osterweil 15). Friedrich built on these conventions that experimental cinema established in the early 1960s. Queer sexuality and experimental practices intersected in restaging the body in vanguard cinema as flamboyant avant-garde director Smith radically reworked camp films from 1950s Hollywood in a language of excess, hyperbole, and shock. For example, in a process that Osterweil calls experimental film's "corporeal mode of address," Smith ruptured the "illusion of cinema's hermetically sealed world" with autobiographical moments in his 1963 film *Blonde Cobra* (3). Experimental cinema implicated bodies of actors, directors, and spectators in aesthetic experiences, in contrast to the practice of Hollywood film to suture a supposedly universal subject into a self-contained fictional world (Osterweil 3).

Cool Hands, Warm Heart integrates diverse visual and tactile conventions of multiple art forms. The film shares with other experimental cinema of the period its existence on a continuum of artistic practices, including performance and body art, sculpture, painting, music, dance, and poetry. Feminist art crosses the classical divisions among painting, sculpture, film, and photography. Partaking in these radical innovations of the 1970s, Friedrich liberates art from the confines of the museum and situates it on densely packed Orchard Street. The women in the film create a network of relations among each other through which they make the private public and move art from the gallery into the street where they circulate among members of diverse class backgrounds.

By the late 1970s, when Friedrich integrated performance art with experimental editing, political activism had made inroads into an understanding of art for a decade. Feminists had rebelled against the marginalization of women artists and demanded a radical change of representation (see also Heartney et al.). Artists asserted themselves vis-à-vis museums and founded the Art Workers Coalition in New York City in the late 1960s (Wark 14). In 1970, after an art strike against Museum of Modern Art (MoMA) in New York City, the journal *Artforum* acknowledged the increasing pressure to engage politics and published a symposium, "The Artist and Politics" (Wark 15). Art became central for second-wave feminists (Phelan 21).

Friedrich's attention to performance art echoed its importance for 1970s feminism. Her work drew on visual arts, theater, dance, music, poetry, and ritual and provided a corporeal language to negotiate art and politics, particularly the dynamics of sexual hierarchy in symbolic and ideological structures of cultural representation (Wark 3). Art historian Moira Roth proclaimed that performance art and the women's movement emerged in the 1960s simultaneously (16). In contrast to the fact that Roth experienced these as mutually reinforcing movements without prehistories, performance art has roots in the cabarets of the late nineteenth and early twentieth centuries, when it influenced avant-garde movements, such as futurism, expressionism, Dadaism, and surrealism, enabling artists to express their visions through their bodies (Wark 29). Such strategies had dispersed artistic expression from the museum to the coffeehouse and the street. In the United States, performance art primarily traces back to 1960s public happenings that involved audience members as participants and gave voice to political protest (Wark 14–15, 30).

Transposing private gestures into the street belonged to the repertoire of a generation of feminist performance artists during the 1960s and 1970s who mobilized their bodies to confront society's expectations of female sexuality in public. Most famously, Austrian Valie Export and American Schneemann used their own nude bodies in their work, shattering taboos, and challenging conventions. Often, their installation work occurred in the context of "expanded cinema," a term that American filmmaker Stan Van Der Beek coined in the mid-1960s and that Gene Youngblood theorized at the beginning of the 1970s in response to the advent of video. In her "Tap and Touch Cinema" ("Tapp und Tastkino" 1968), for example, Export carried a box in front of her naked breasts and encouraged strangers to reach in and touch them. Similarly, Schneemann, in her most famous performance piece, pulled a paper scroll out of her vagina and read it on stage. Friedrich's work also embraces the low-budget, homemade aesthetic that defines Export's cardboard box and Schneemann's paper scroll. Such artistic practices created an audience familiar with intermedial art production for Friedrich's film.

The performances in *Cool Hands, Warm Heart* enact the production of femininity. By staging the intimate processes of womanhood, such as shaving legs and underarms, in the public place of a busy street, the film points to the cultural processes that delineate the female body. For men, the beard symbolizes masculinity, maturity, and status. For women, the presumed lack of body hair situates them in a binary relationship to men, suggesting an animalistic proximity for masculinity and an approximation of prepubescent girlhood for femininity, turning youth and its lack of power into attractive attributes. The culture of grooming projects onto women the heterosexual desire to appeal to men. Simultaneously, because the hairless female body should appear natural, the intimate labor of self-fashioning should be invisible. Butler's later concept of performativity decodes this process, arguing that foregrounding the acts of creating gender exposes the fantasy of its biological foundation.

Second-wave feminism ascertained that beauty conventions oppressed women. The synecdoche of bra-burning emblematizes the radical destruction of feminine appearance, part of the second women's movement's "sex-gender system," which considered sex the biological ground and gender its interpretation. In contrast, queer studies posits that gender imposes the lens through which to read sex. Friedrich's films enable us to focus less on the paradigm shift from feminism to queer theory and more on the continuity by attending to the performativity of femininity and the disentangling of desire from presumed heterosexuality. Even if scholars have revealed bra-burning as reductive history of the second women's movement, such a symbol, nevertheless, captures the force that inheres in transforming intimate self-fashioning into public rebellion.

Later queer theory thematizes performativity, while transgender studies offers phenomenological approaches to the body, continuing the focus on the lived reality of "genders beyond the binary of male and female" (Salamon 6). Scholar of transgender studies Gayle Salamon, for example, emphasizes the coexistence of the biological and social body but challenges the notion of unmediated access to the former. Thus, she theorizes the gendered body in ways that continue consideration initiated in this earlier moment (1). Salamon emphasizes the forces that shape bodies, including the gender binary, which occur across a matrix of instruments, techniques, and procedures (76–80). *Cool Hands, Warm Heart* begins Friedrich's exploration of the body as a site shaped by experience and power.

This reading of Friedrich's early work, foregrounding the generative force of her feminist experimental cinema, contrasts with projections of essentialism onto second-wave feminism from a twenty-first-century vantage point. For example, performance scholar Rebecca Schneider correctly argues that sexuality was a central feature in experimental cinema and performance art of the 1970s in a throughline from artist Schneemann's *Eye/Body* (1963) to the early 1990s works of porn artist Annie Sprinkle and performance artist Karen Finley. At the same time, Schneider accuses second-wave feminism as having been too essentialist to recognize this subversive practice (2). In particular, she charges the magazine for which Friedrich worked with misreading such subversive art, calling its makers "[r]igidly essentialist feminists, such as the *Heresies* collective in the 1960s [*sic*]" (37). As the journal had a publication run from 1977 to 1993 and did not yet exist in the 1960s, such criticism reveals the projection of essentialism onto second-wave feminists as a precondition for the claim of sexual transgression for later feminist and queer theory.

Orchard Street

Cool Hands, Warm Heart's politics of location inserts the film into a metadiscourse on avant-garde cinema. The film's setting of Orchard Street carries additional meaning as an emblematic site for New York City experimental cinema and adds layers to its film history. As part of Manhattan's Lower East Side, Orchard Street was the unofficial base of experimental cinema in New York City, a magnet for avant-garde writers and a location for misfits, as well as a home to immigrants and discount shopping. Orchard Street covers eight city blocks between Division

Street in Chinatown and East Houston Street on the Lower East Side. The iconic street was significant for avant-garde film culture beginning in the 1950s and throughout the 1970s. In 1953, when director Mekas left the Lithuanian immigrant community in Brooklyn, he moved to 95 Orchard Street, where he published the journal *Film Culture* with his brother Adolfas (Mekas, "Few Notes" 97–98). Their film workshop later turned into the Anthology Film Archives. Around another corner, the Millennium was located on 66 East Fourth Street. In short, the Lower East Village was a "hotbed of counterculture artistic and political activity" where a group of filmmakers declared the birth of the New American Cinema on September 28, 1960 (Galm 102). Those "beatniks, bohemians, leftist intellectuals, anarchists, poets, artists, queers, utopians," who famously included Allen Ginsberg and Jack Kerouac, were directors, actors, and audience members of films (Koponen 113). Brick tenement buildings with fire escapes characterize the neighborhood, immortalized in the Lower East Side Tenement Museum, which showcases the history of generations of immigrants.[5] The densely populated district provided the backdrop of canonical films, such as *The Jazz Singer* (1927) and *The Naked City* (1948) (Meyerling 107).

By situating the action in Orchard Street, *Cool Hands, Warm Heart* references the past history of film and conjures up the urban geography of experimental cinema and its canon. Spectators who belonged to the New York City experimental-film scene would have recognized Orchard Street and its significance, as it evokes Jacobs's film of the eponymous title *Orchard Street* (1955). Jacobs, founder of the Millennium Workshop and the Film Studies Department at Binghamton University, made *Orchard Street* in 1955 with a 16 mm Bell & Howell camera.[6] It shows the one-way street with a line of traffic and pedestrians spilling from the sidewalks into the street. Friedrich's insertion of female performance art via *Cool Hands, Warm Heart* into this particular street, the symbolic site of experimental cinema, therefore, takes on added meaning.

Scratching

While the location provides realistic, symbolic, and metareflective meaning, the film exceeds its realism of on-location shooting through its enigmatic and dreamlike poetics. The scratched text radically changes the point of view from an observational stance to a subjective perspective.

For example, the text reads: "In a house, a tree, it shattered the windows impaled the inhabitants rotted the foundation but as it tore through the roof I woke myself up." The direct manipulation of the celluloid through scratching results in flickering text on the screen where the words appear intermittently with a disregard of grammar to evoke mental images. Instead of illuminating the action, the text's poetic register contributes an enigmatic layer to the performance. It adds a narrative subjective voice unmoored from the realist time and space, free floating and unrelated to any of the characters. It begins with individual words, "Disarm" and "Alarm," and moves to questions and statements with an I-narrator. In all capital letters, the text spans several frames: "can i stop them" and "if i can't stop." Short phrases ask questions of spectators. The fragments do not cohere to a whole but evoke a narrator distinct from the women that appear on the screen. Instead of the illusion of a cohesive and embodied voice, the characters appear in mute performances on screen with fragmented and interspersed subjective I-narrations inscribed into the film. Those scratched texts, therefore, suggest a biographical dimension without ever confirming such a link. The subjective text also emphasizes the materiality of the medium. Documenting a busy street, the film invites audience members to connect art as embodied practice to the perception of film as mediation that circulates publicly. The unstable continuity of images that results from the manipulation of individual frames evokes early cinema as the visible individual shots remind spectators that the optical illusion of film results from sequential images, which the eye and the human brain perceive as movement.

The scratching retains the trace of the director as author and gives this film a haptic dimension. This quality connects the materiality of the film to the diegesis—the women touching themselves and each other. The handholds and public intimacy of the women estrange the small gestures and habits of femininity and explode the heterosexual contract in the public realm. The film offers a future vision for women as they establish a network of erotic and desirous relations among each other in public. Following experimental cinema's ability to "overcome the boundaries between self and other," *Cool Hands, Warm Heart* creates a complex network among subjectivity, medium, and performance art (Osterweil 11).

Avant La Lettre

Few scholars paid attention to *Cool Hands, Warm Heart* before the emergence of queer theory. Early critical supporters of Friedrich's experimental filmmaking, such as film scholars Lindley Hanlon and Scott MacDonald, reacted to what they perceived as radical feminism. Hanlon penned the first article on Friedrich's early films in the *Millennium Film Journal* (1982–1983) in spring 1983. Shots from Friedrich's *Gently Down the Stream* and "Regional Reports—Feminism" on the 1983 cover of the journal demonstrate that feminist filmmaking was gaining prominence, while Hanlon's title "Female Rage: The Films of Su Friedrich" captures the perception of feminist film at the time. Hanlon claims that the daily rituals the women in the film perform, such as shaving legs and underarms, "look like bizarre, sado-masochistic acts" (80). She criticizes the film for lacking aesthetics, sensuality, visual play, choreography, and pretty images. She concludes that rage defines the action as the on-screen women express negative emotions, such as anger and pain, in their faces. In addition, she views the scratched script as an act of violence against the celluloid strip and by implication against the spectator (80). Similarly, MacDonald, who importantly advanced the study of independent and experimental film, in general, and Friedrich's oeuvre, in particular, over the span of her career, suggests that *Cool Hands, Warm Heart* advances a "grim feminism" ("Su Friedrich" 283). In a 1988 interview, he shared that he found *Scar Tissue* and *Cool Hands, Warm Heart* "hard to look at," as they seemed to be made as "as feminist exercises" ("Damned" 6). The scholars' perceptions of rage and grimness respond to the film's refusal of femininity and its embrace of feminism, indicating broader societal and scholarly reservations at the time.

The film's subtle performance of butchness shatters taboos not only for mainstream audiences but also among feminists at the time. The unnamed main character who moves through the crowd inhabits a defiant pose and look in the film's opening. Her strong, wide-legged stance and direct look at the camera refuses postures of femininity. The second-wave women's movement denounced butch and femme, the subcultural expression of lesbian sexuality particularly pronounced in the 1940s and 1950s, as retrograde because of its embrace of masculine style, which second-wave feminism perceived as emulating patriarchal power. As Friedrich herself describes in "Renegades: Butches and Studs, in Their

Own Words," a *New York Times* video published in April 2020, feminists in the 1970s and 1980s considered those lesbian social identities old-fashioned and sometimes even reactionary. Butch-femme aesthetics resurfaced throughout the 1990s as a form of performative camp instead of a style born out of the need for survival.

In the late 1990s, queer-studies scholar Jack Halberstam suggests that both patriarchal heterosexism and second-wave feminism and womanism vilified female masculinity as a pathological misidentification with heterosexual patriarchy (*Masculinity* 9). *Cool Hands, Warm Heart*'s main female figure, who eschews femininity and enacts a masculine cool pose, disavows expectations of normalized femininity, including the accommodating smile. Yet, the character relates intimately to the other women, including riding off on a bicycle in the film's conclusion. Halberstam defines masculinity as a construction that female-born as well as male-born people could inhabit (*Masculinity* 13). The woman in the film acts authentically when she performs a masculine habitus such as taking up space while moving through the crowd, while the others highlight gestures of femininity when they perform rites of womanhood on their makeshift pedestals. In the complex interplay of acting naturally and performing gender, the film reverses assumptions about biological sex.[7]

New Queer Cinema

Friedrich's work, including *Cool Hands, Warm Heart*, garnered increased attention with the emergence of New Queer Cinema in the early 1990s. Queer-film theorists recognized her films' vanguard quality but simultaneously regarded her lesbian identification as out of step in the newly arising paradigms of queerness. "Queer" had been a rallying cry in response to the AIDS epidemic, when gay, lesbian, bisexual, and transgender activists embraced and appropriated the previously derogatory label. Mobilizing the term for political action and cultural expression entailed a double move: it gathered nonnormative sexualities under a single umbrella term and simultaneously subverted notions of coherent identity. Journalist and scholar B. Ruby Rich coined the term "New Queer Cinema" in her eponymous 1992 essay when she noticed the high number of queer filmmakers and their films at festivals that year. Most of the filmmakers, except for British director Derek Jarman, belonged to a younger generation that arrived at film festivals with their first films: Gregg Araki, Benning, Haynes, Isaac Julien, Kalin, and Jennie Livingstone (Rich, "New"). Directors, such as Friedrich, Hammer, and Ahwesh, did not fit the mold. In response to this perception of new talent, scholarship exploded between 1990 and 1993. Books on gay and lesbian films (Dyer; Weiss) and scholarship on queer cinema (Bad Object-Choices; Gever et al.) appeared in quick succession in three years, transforming the field from an analysis of stereotypes of gay and lesbian representation to queer deconstructive and psychoanalytic readings that herald subversive aesthetics.

Scholars turned to Friedrich's work in the context of queer cinema but projected her films into an earlier era, subsequently casting them as a precursor of New Queer Cinema. Nevertheless, her cinema suddenly commanded attention with the emerging field of queer films studies and its accompanying expanding audiences. Scholars, such as art historian Liz Kotz, appreciated the nonnarrative strategies of *Cool Hands, Warm Heart* and acknowledged that Friedrich enhanced the tradition of American avant-garde filmmaking with her poetic style, recognizing the deconstructive possibility of experimental cinema for a new queer imaginary (95). Kotz contextualized film's "lesbian representation" among the works of other prominent experimental directors, such as Child and Cecilia Dougherty, and took recourse to Butler's 1990 *Gender Trouble* as a theoretical framework to analyze Friedrich's provocative formal aesthetics in contrast to other previous positive and commodified lesbian erotic images (87).

Queer studies focused on the discursive production of sexual identities and staged its intervention as overcoming what it cast as the essentialism of cultural feminism and gay liberation (Samer 8). As a result, the new scholarship linked queerness to performativity and deviance and cast the lesbian feminist as "an anachronistic drag" (Samer 9). Queer studies distinguished itself from social movements that preceded it and consequently subsumed lesbians in the category of "queer" (Keller 5). Recent rethinking of that relationship, however, for example, in a study of lesbian film after queer theory, suggests that the "combined histories of queer and lesbian as terms of attachment and political motivation have run not only in parallel but through mutual constitution" (Bradbury-Rance 10). Yet, importantly, queer theorists recognized how *Cool Hands,*

Warm Heart forged the confluence of performance art and feminist sensibility in the public sphere to challenge notions of female gender and foreground its performative quality.

Gendered Mobility

Friedrich's next film, *Scar Tissue*, privileges formal editing patterns to highlight binary genders of masculine and feminine in everyday performances that otherwise go unnoticed. The film repeats and varies footage, mostly of feet, that Friedrich shot of men and women walking, standing, and rushing (figure 3). The six-minute, black-and-white silent film, shot on Super 8 mm and 16 mm, captures the evocative shadows that lighting produces in black-and-white celluloid film.[8] With *Scar Tissue*, Friedrich, who completes all aspects of production and postproduction of her films, demonstrates her deep commitment to editing, which continues throughout her career and led up to the 2019 creation of a website of women editors.[9] Her ability to foreground graphic patterns in *Scar Tissue* relies on shooting material of observational quality with an eye to

Figure 3. Waiting and walking
in *Scar Tissue* (1979)

composition. This film, then, results from a personal archive of unique footage that focuses on fragments of bodies in business attire, including feet and legs, as well as lower and midsection part of bodies, most often in solitary positions but also standing and moving in small groups.

Scar Tissue invites kinetic responses without presenting characters for identification. Postures and gestures mark gender differences. The opening shot shows two men self-confidently asserting space, one of them smiling flirtatiously and winking at the camera presumably carried by a woman. This tiny gesture, easily missed, inscribes the camerawoman into the gendered relationship between the carrier of the gaze and its object. Whereas, following Mulvey, the camera objectifies the human character on screen, here the gendered reversal—male object and female carrier of the gaze—allows the man to assert his power even from an object position to reverse and objectify the presumed woman behind the camera through an implicit assertion of heterosexual agreement: the wink. Bodies, mostly in medium long shots, relate to each other spatially, standing or moving. Men in relaxed postures talk to each other with expansive and assertive gestures that express confidence and power. Men and women walk, stand, and move through urban space. Again, Friedrich scratches the title *Scar Tissue* into the film and, thus, creates a haptic effect.

Scar Tissue exposes the restrictions that femininity imposes on women's mobility. The images of women's feet moving through the urban environment increase through the course of the film and their presence creates an independent kinetic rhythm beyond the previously dominating presence of men. Images become more dynamic as shots capture rapid movements in different directions. Corporeality constitutes the film's material without the fetishization that traditionally characterizes shots of women's body parts. Female figures are standing or moving furtively across shots, rushing here or there in high-heeled pumps or sandals with straps. In instances, compositions marginalize feet at the periphery of the frame. The quick sequences challenge audience perception and comprehension. Throughout the film, editing contrasts shots of static bodies with others in motion. In addition, the film cuts shots on movement, left to right and vice versa, such that they cohere into patterns of varying graphic match cuts. Compositions of bodies that relate to each other within and across shots assume an architectural quality. In instances, a white screen flashes in between black screens, emphasizing the film's structural and abstract quality that privileges rhythm. The imagery serves as raw material for a patterning that subtly rearranges the structures of gendered power relations over the course of the film. Instead of editing to establish the illusion of a continuous time and space, it precludes identification with characters. *Scar Tissue*'s rejection of character identification and its nuanced foregrounding of gendered embodiment distinguish it from militant feminist and queer cinema of the time, such as the classic *Born in Flames* (Lizzie Borden, 1983), which famously portrayed groups of feminists fighting for the revolution.[10]

Scar Tissue captures how the traditional two-gender system organizes action and perception in the public sphere. Friedrich's montage of shots contrasts the everyday apparel, movement, embodiment, and spatial politics of men and women. The formal composition offers a structural analysis, subversion, and critique of binary gender. Women's feet appear in delicate shoes with patterns. One shot reveals a woman standing still on her high heels on a step that implies an invisible imposing building, while a man walks by leisurely. A slight, almost indiscernible lift in the woman's right foot hints at the way women pose instead of grounding their feet solidly.

Scar Tissue begins with a black screen, and subsequently individual shots flash on the screen. Instead of a classic montage pattern of shot A, shot B, shot C, the black screen separates shots. Their brevity challenges cognitive perceptions. As the film continues, the shot length increases, which enables audiences to recognize individual content. Images and sequences repeat, permitting viewers to perceive their content—feet standing in the street, women walking—based on previous content. That way, the film continuously estranges and recontextualizes while upending traditional conventions of leftist cinema. Friedrich's editing neither aims for visual pleasure moving toward synthesis, typical for collage, nor does it use dialectics to create a synthesis as in montage. Rather, the continuing emphasis on contrast while withholding resolution forces audiences to register the underlying gender binary through the process of watching the film.

The seemingly prosaic activities of standing and walking expose the dominant construction of gender in the late 1970s. A shot shows a

woman remaining stationary in the foreground, while the man dynami-
cally strides across the shot, passing her, and by extension the audience,
without hesitation. His movement signals purpose and direction, while
the woman's immobility suggests posing and waiting. The latter became
a central topic for feminist art in the 1970s. Artist Faith Wilding, for
example, created and performed a piece in 1972, "Waiting," in which
she recited a poem about the different phases of waiting in women's
lives (Roth 144–45). Friedrich herself entered a debate about women
and waiting in a letter to the editor about West German feminist director Margarethe von Trotta's *Second Awakening of Christa Klages* (1978)
("Letters").[11] Responding to the question whether the film's main female
character had waited too long or not long enough, Friedrich references
Odysseus instead of Penelope, the icon of female waiting ("Letters" 42).
Far from validating waiting as female activity, Friedrich advocates for
women to assert agency and embrace mobility.

Repetition

Individual shots reoccur as part of the film's rhythm and pattern, which
denaturalizes the action on screen. Limiting the number of different
images underscores the reappearance of individual images as well as
variation among similar ones. Friedrich mobilizes film's reproducibil-
ity in her use of duplicate material, which challenges viewers to view
the same images anew. By reusing shots, Friedrich draws spectators'
attention to the reiteration of actions, behaviors, and gestures. Through
replicating variations of action, such as posing and waiting or gesturing
and moving, Friedrich trains an audience to perceive the inscription
of gender in the everyday. Friedrich's rhythmic editing pattern rearranges the relationship between traditional gender categories without
advancing a claim for radical revolution. Friedrich abnegates familiar
political rhetoric, such as visible didacticisms, explicit explanation, or
call to action. The film expresses its politics through editing and lack of
resolution to subvert the status of gender as natural.

Friedrich's attention to the reiteration of gender performance finds
a theoretical equivalency in Butler's later revision of second-wave feminism's sex/gender system in which sex was the biological "truth" and
gender its cultural interpretation. More than a decade after *Cool Hands,
Warm Heart* and *Scar Tissue*, Butler accords repetition a crucial role in

her argument about the performativity of gender. She explains, "Rules that are partially structured along matrices of gender hierarchy and compulsory heterosexuality, operate through *repetition*" (145, italics in original). She argues that repetition also has the capacity to make the performative nature of gender visible and, thus, subvert the notion of biological identity, a process that Friedrich's film advances. Images of men in the center with women surrounding them dominate the first half of the film. However, as the film progresses, more shots with women appear until their presence outnumbers that of men. The shift suggests a growing presence of women in the public sphere, which affects spectators unconsciously as the film does not use any documentary conventions to make this claim. The use of white screens and black screens in the film's opening and closing sections invites spectators to reflect on what they see.

The editing underscores the fact that cognition of one image inflects the observation of the next. An audience comprehends images of "women" in contrast to the images of "men," while movement in one shot heightens awareness of stillness in another. Russian director Lev Kuleshov studied how an audience's reactions to one image influence their reading of the subsequent shots. In the famous experiment of the Kuleshov effect during the late 1910s and early 1920s, he intercut a straight-on shot of a man looking at the camera with three other shots, that of a dead child, a bowl of soup, and a beautiful woman. Kuleshov proposed that spectators perceive the man's face differently in each context, projecting sadness onto the face associated with the dead child, hunger onto the expression when tethered to the soup, and finally desire when preceding the image of the beautiful woman. *Scar Tissue*'s editing foregrounds the contrast between men and women and points to the binary construction of gender. The notion of women's presence in space inflects the audience's perception of men's mobility. Whereas gender appears to be natural and coincidental at the film's outset, the repetition of the gestures and movement and the editing that foregrounds contrast and similarity highlight the enactment and artificiality of gender by the film's conclusion.

Through the experience of viewing, audience members may grasp that in the binary gender system, the notion of one gender inflects that of the other. Women appear in opposition to men, and men become visible in distinction to women. Relaxed men with their hands in their pockets, talking, and gesticulating with a cigar, contrast to women's feet moving from here to there and vanishing out of the picture. The relaxed dominance of masculinity only becomes visible through the cinematic strategies of repetition and cross-cutting. Repeatedly, the camera looks down on the women's shoes and offers up-canted shots or straight-on shots on the men. Particularly in the opening, Friedrich layers images of men with their briefcases, increasing the number of shots that encapsulate such professional habitus before and after images of women, which creates a sense of an overwhelming presence of men in the public. The multiplication of shots draws attention to their habits and reveals the performances that produce masculinity.

Experimental Dreamscapes

Friedrich's film *Gently Down the Stream* (1981) initiates the autobiographical turn in her work to become a thread throughout the majority of her oeuvre. Advancing her avant-garde experimental editing, the film continues her focus on gendered imaginary with an explicit subjective position about female sexuality. *Gently Down the Stream* expresses intimate feelings and experiences, specifically of her dreams. She garnered prominence with *Gently Down the Stream* as her breakthrough film when scholars, critics, and audiences celebrated its enigmatic beauty. The film catapulted Friedrich beyond the circle of experimental filmmakers in the Lower East Side of New York City and onto film festivals and college campuses. It expresses several of Friedrich's own dreams in experimental film language. The formal quality consists of scratching of words over images. Vignettes create phantasmatic atmospheric dreamscapes across clusters of images that inflect each other. Explicit sexual references, such as "orgasm," "vagina," and "pubic hair," for example, assert the female subject as both articulating desire and being the object of erotic yearning. The footage includes iconic images that run through Friedrich's oeuvre: pictures of the Madonna and women swimming or entering and exiting pools. Friedrich explained this practice in an interview: "By scratching words onto the screen and combining them with images that were only tangentially related to the dream text, I wanted to create that sense of dislocation that one has when one tries to recall a dream—the feeling that one's simple verbal description of 'what happened' never quite captures the elusive, convoluted, and illogical narrative that one experienced while dreaming" (Muhlstein 58). Including the title, *Gently Down the Stream*, the film invokes a soothing atmosphere, while its explicit and taboo-breaking language overlays nonsexual imagery.

The film's flow of images and associative texts create a dreamlike quality. The grammatically incorrect writing, scratched into the celluloid, addresses spectators with evocative commands. The film opens with a text that provides a sense of moving through space without precise referentialities: "Wander through / large quiet / rooms." Reenacting the experience of film projection, Friedrich employs the rolling image of the Madonna, an icon of Catholicism. Once the image becomes stable and an audience can identify the face of the statue, it does not carry obvious meaning in the context of other images and the text, thus being emotionally evocative. To the contrary, the familiar icon challenges spectators to reflect on the link between image and signification.

Friedrich's emphasis on dreams illuminates why the combinations of texts and images simultaneously acquire and evade meaning. In addition to her film, Friedrich printed a small booklet in 1982 that includes images and poetics from *Gently Down the Stream*. A brief explanation at the end of the booklet states that text and images from the film correlate to each passage in the book as a separate dream. Friedrich had reproduced texts from her journals and included them out of order of the chronology in which she had experienced them. She sums up her method as follows: "When you watch the film, you read the dream" (Private collection of Su Friedrich).

The film includes connections that in dreams appear to make sense. In one example, this text appears on screen: "An old friend says what are you doing here? I say the weavers worked as slaves to make these rugs. Think / worked as slaves / she shouts." Friedrich concludes the series of rolling and arrested images of the Madonna with a grainy close-up shot that evokes the famous image of experimental filmmaker Maya Deren holding her hand against the glass and creating a mirroring reflection in *Meshes in the Afternoon* (1943). The shot pays homage to the predecessor who advanced surrealist visions. As if to comment ironically on such a possible reference, the sequence concludes with the line: "This is pure civilization."

Gently Down the Stream's different linguistic and visual experiences create a phantasmatic whole that invites audience members to participate in collective associative processes of remembering. From the beginning of cinema, dreams provided an important narrative trope. They appeared in early silent cinema, which later attracted the midcentury French avant-garde to what film-studies scholar Tom Gunning called "the cinema of attractions" (see "Attractions"). Friedrich does not limit images and words to those that evoke a positive affect. In contrast, she confronts the audience with a second-person address: "Why do you come here and spoil everything?" The question and its implied accusation that the addressee ruins pleasurable events invoke Sara Ahmed's concept of the "feminist killjoy," the person that questions seeming harmony by pointing to the underlying injustice on which the status quo is predicated (see *Living*). The different emotions that the film conjures up without privileging one over the other asks spectators to remember their own dreams.

At the intersection of religion and desire, the film articulates female subjectivity by combining and contrasting familiar images, such as the Madonna, with Friedrich's intimate memories of her mother and fantasies of female sexuality. Throughout her career, Friedrich repeatedly returned to Catholicism, as it is central to the repression of sexuality but, therefore, also provides a vehicle to retrieve the repressed. In the film's early text—"Walk into church my mother trembles trances reciting a prayer about orgasm I start to weep"—Friedrich intercuts shots of a woman's feet working out on a cardio rowing machine (figure 4). This brief textual interlude connects the transcendence of religious belief and sexual experience, which the text resolves in tears. After its conclusion, another shot presents the woman sitting in the rowing machine from a different angle, capturing the self-disciplining of women's bodies.

In several of the film's sections, intriguing tension arises from incongruous combinations of intimate accounts that give shape to feelings and from images of women's body parts and everyday mundane activities. Text and image-track appear in a contrapuntal composition. *Gently Down the Stream*'s episodic structure likens to the paratactic organization of early silent cinema. Without a narrative with cause-and-effect logic, sequences could be exchanged with each other. Text and images provoke associations, for example, in sections showing women using

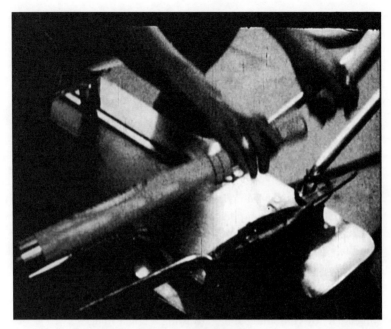

Figure 4. Rowing in *Gently Down
the Stream* (1981)

a rowing machine and entering a water basin. The text dominates the screen, which includes a white square: "In the water near a raft I see a woman swimming and diving in a wet suit see her pubic hair a woman sits on a stage hunched over in the corner she calls up a friend from the audience asking her Come and make love to me She does I can't watch." The writing overlays images of a woman in a "wifebeater" shirt who begins to row. The final text, "She mutters I can't can't hold you The last time was too tense so many memories," accompanies footage of a woman's feet walking into a water basin in a swimming-pool hall. Women inhabit active bodies that engage physically in all kinds of environments, swimming, walking, riding a bicycle, exercising, and driving. Friedrich's female characters reject traditional femininity. The rowing woman's butchness reveals itself in her clothing, haircut, and motion.

Friedrich eschews the normative expectation that an explanatory text should illuminate the visual track. Instead, she insists on the associative potential of enigmatic texts: "Woman on the bed shivers I wake her she is angry smears spermicidal jelly on my lips No!" A woman entering a pool accompanies the text, continuing the theme of female bodies in the public space. The references to lesbian desire infuse the everyday images. Poetic texts are sometimes written onto images, sometimes narrated in the voice-over. Traditionally, text dominates the image as filmmakers use voice-over or writing to illuminate the image track. In *Gently Down the Stream*, the enigmatic text and images rub off on each other without completing a dialectic or a supplementary relationship. The scratched text poses a cognitive challenge to spectators because individual words appear in separate shots, slowing the pace of reading. A single word appears without a context to suggest meaning. Rhythmic pattern and increased pacing heighten the emotional address.

The film includes compositional elements reminiscent of structural and abstract cinema. A white screen in the top right announces a new sequence. Incomplete sentences, grammatical inaccuracies, and negative commands intrigue: "Building a model house for some man Do it without getting paid Do it wrong." Friedrich's use of different squares on the screen evokes early abstract film with mobile shapes, such as squares, triangles, and circles. Friedrich blends such figurations with concrete language and realistic footage.

The evocative poetic text stops short of cohering into comprehensible meaning. Ignoring grammatical rules, it invokes unbound and unfocused desire: "I draw a man take his skin inflate it get excited mount it. It's like being in love with a straight woman." Images of water, which return in point-of-view shots from a moving ferry, intercut with abstractions, also dissolve boundaries. Friedrich provides a narration from a dream over an image of the crest of an ocean wave: "I lie in a gutter giving birth to myself two fetuses dark green and knotted up Try to breathe so they don't suffocate I can pull one out, but it starts to crumble up." Calming water evokes the embryonic state and regression associated with dreams. The film advances with increasing absurdity referencing the failure of linguistic translation: "Five women sing in acapella funny harmony they spell the word truth in German I spell blindness A man says Their Song is a very Clever Pun I say I can't agree I don't know German."

In the film's conclusion, Friedrich dissolves the subjectivity of the narrator among the images and bodies and increases the onomatopoeic quality, emphasizing sound qualities over semantic meaning. The text turns into wordplay about animals in a pure fantasy of affects without coherent meaning for the scene it evokes: "A leopard A leopard eats two blue hummingbirds I feel the feathers utter flutter on my bones mutter hearts utter feathers humming on my tongue." Individual shots combine scratched words and images to challenge audiences to relate them to each other (figure 5). When the text rhymes "utter," "flutter" and "mutter," it transforms words into a sensory experience of language devoid of meaning.

Critical Success

The invocation of dreams, closely related to mythical and psychological thinking, made *Gently Down the Stream* recognizable and readable as experimental cinema in the context of Sitney's "visionary film." By the mid-to-late 1970s, New American Cinema shifted from an allegiance to its European precursors to what Sitney described as "the triumph

Figure 5. Su Friedrich scratching the print
of *Gently Down the Stream* (1981), originally
in color. Image courtesy Su Friedrich

of the imagination," which offers a lens to read and understand Friedrich's film. The trance film, from Cocteau's *Le Sang d'un Poète* (1932) to Deren's *Meshes of the Afternoon* (1943), played a central role in his understanding of visionary film (18). *Gently Down the Stream* creates such a sensory experience.

Critics celebrated Friedrich's transformation of dream fragments into film (Hanlon 83). Hanlon perceptively identifies a development to a more subjective mode in Friedrich's filmmaking that shifts from a focus on the external world to images of an internal vision. The scholar views women as caught between conventional expectations and the search for liberation and highlights the image in the film in which Friedrich envisions giving birth to herself as expressing emancipation. The emphasis on the dream for Hanlon situates Friedrich in the context of the avant-garde's "personal psycho-cinema" (83).

In *Gently Down the Stream*, Friedrich's editing method allows open-ended connections, emotions, and reflections to arise for audience members. She invites spectators to experience the pleasure of the disavowal that is typical of dreams and the cinema: "I know it is not real, but I enjoy it as if it were real nevertheless." This dreamlike state has been particularly pronounced in the work of experimental filmmakers, such that Sitney enshrined it as the aesthetic paradigms of the American avant-garde, especially the works of experimental filmmakers Brakhage, Mekas, and Frampton. Through the combination of enigmatic poetry with rhythmic editing, Friedrich creates an intensely personal film distinct from her previous works that sets the stage for later films to come.

Gendered Labor

But No One (1982) completes the cycle of Friedrich's early abstract experimental films. Its strong connection to *Scar Tissue* also demonstrates that while Friedrich advances a coherent style across her oeuvre and develops different emphases throughout her career, from performance art to abstract editing to subjective dreamscapes, she does not advance her artistic vision in a linear chronology. Repeatedly throughout her career she explores new themes and aesthetic strategies only to take up the practices and topics from her previous films. Thus, Friedrich not only resists the categories of genre but also predictability of her artistic development.

But No One relies heavily on editing and subtly addresses a feminist concern with work—a social issue instead of a subjective one. The film rhythmically combines images that contrast masculine and feminine spheres. The nine-minute, black-and-white film interweaves three main image tracks: men in hard hats toiling on a demolition site of a building in New York City; a woman working as a prostitute in the street, shot from above a rooftop; and shots of a fish market. Friedrich adds to these recurring visual threads short sequences of a female and a male nude, a woman getting into a bathtub, water, and firefighters. As is her practice, Friedrich shot the footage for the film herself, imbuing the material with the qualities that become manifest through the editing process. One of the key aspects of the film is, therefore, the gendered nature of its footage. The men in hard hats at work move about on a construction site, seemingly unaware of being filmed. Their presence indicates how traditional imaginary naturalizes the conflation of masculinity and manual labor. In contrast, a long shot from the top of the building shows a woman in the street below. It takes some time to comprehend the nature of her interaction with men in cars. As a prostitute, she must be simultaneously visible—to attract customers—and invisible—to avoid law enforcement. The repetition of her gestures, approaching cars, talking, and stepping back reveals her activity not as waiting for a friend but negotiating sexual and monetary transactions. Friedrich's editing intercuts these occupations that occur in the space of legality and visibility and illegality and invisibility. In the third image track, fish flush through an opening and appear at a fish stand at the market (figure 6).

Continuing her strategy from previous films, Friedrich uses repetition and variation to enable the audience first to recognize the gendered specificity and then slowly to understand the production of gender and its perception. By containing men in one set of shots and women in another, Friedrich creates a gendered but not heterosexual archive of images, which connects *But No One* to *Scar Tissue*. In classic cinema, normative binary gender and heterosexuality mutually reinforce one another and coincide when the narrative concludes with the happy ending of the straight couple—traditionally joined in the final shot. With *But No One*, Friedrich refuses such a conclusion. The images of fish rejects the expectations either to offer the dialectical resolution of montage or the typical narrative trajectory of the heterosexual gendered classic

Figure 6. Fish in *But No One* (1982).
Image courtesy Su Friedrich

conclusion. The film does not resolve existing contradictions of gendered labor in the public sphere.

Similar to the dreamscapes of *Gently Down the Stream*, Friedrich scratched an enigmatic text into celluloid. Grammatically incorrect, its evocative and open-ended wordplay aims at an affective response by audience members: "Dark sky fat boy Crash shadow waves water fat boy on a ledge crash shadow lurch waves water fat boy on a ledge women stand grief stricken by the canal babies of all races float by in colorful clothes all dead or dying little mouths." The text's poetic devices—homonyms, assonances, alliterations, repetitions, and duplications—have aural qualities and pertain to the text's rhythmic pattern. The language inflects the images with a sense of anxiety and dread. As in her earlier films, the scratched text creates an associative connection to the visuals, which neither include a "fat boy" nor a "woman on the ledge." The repetition invokes prelinguistic mental images of floating and fluidity that transcend the realistic footage of the film and counters the notion of the written text as precise information. Instead, text, through the scratching associated with the haptic, addresses audiences' associative and affective registers. As a result, the fish gasping for air appears desperate, the men on the construction site seem in danger, and the woman working the street appears downtrodden. The film captures gendered labor but moves beyond the social discourse associated with work into a poetic, yet uncertain, realm.

In turning to Friedrich's oeuvre, in general, and emphasizing her early films here, in particular, this volume seeks to capture the aesthetics that second-wave feminism ushered into film, the art world, and, thus, the public sphere. From the outset, a focus on gender and sexuality defines Friedrich's cinema. Her films question dominant narratives and generate alternative visions. Returning to her early films from the vantage point of the twenty-first century allows continuities among feminist, queer, and transgender culture, activism, and theory to come into view, in contrast to an emphasis on ruptures, conflicts, and breaks. *Gently Down the Stream*'s radical articulation of her own subjectivity anticipates her next set of films, in which she explicitly addresses memory and history through her autobiography, beginning with her relationship to her mother.

Counter Memories

During the 1980s Friedrich's experimental strategies focus on memory. Her films assert the validity of previously marginalized emotions, embodiments, and desires in the construction of a public sphere that imagines a future for women, lesbians, and queers who happen to be mothers, daughters, and lovers. The three films that Friedrich makes during the decade create an alternative archive to hegemonic history. She forges a cinematic language that engages processes of remembering. Following her short experimental films of the late 1970s and early 1980s, she expands the length of her films with three titles three years apart. Friedrich mobilizes her biography for films that integrate conventions of narrative, documentary, and avant-garde cinema.

Friedrich concentrates on her relationship to her mother in *The Ties That Bind* (1984) and to her father in *Sink or Swim* (1990), while *Damned If You Don't* (1987) expands the focus on memory by articulating a collective lesbian subjectivity, organized around the figure of the nun as an object of desire. In *The Ties That Bind*, Friedrich dialogically examines her mother's life in shared remembrances, while in *Sink or Swim* she poetically works through her relationship with her father. Friedrich's artistic evocations of the past in the present occur a decade before memory studies intensifies. This expansive field reflects a cultural shift in response to demands by previously ignored groups for representation in the archives of official history.

Friedrich's integration of subjective memory and feminist-lesbian politics offers intimate portraits and conjures up community. Her films of this period defy classification as they integrate experimental, narrative, and documentary characteristics, including aspects of the diary film, most famously associated with experimental filmmaker Mekas. Avant-garde filmmakers during the 1970s and 1980s rejected the personal cinema of Brakhage and Mekas, as well as the structural films by Michael Snow and Paul Sharits (MacDonald, "Su Friedrich: *Ties*" 102). Friedrich consolidates "traditionally distinct arenas of independent film" by reappropriating and reenergizing these previous experimental practices to integrate the personal and the systematic (MacDonald, "Su Friedrich: *Ties*" 103).

Throughout the 1980s and into the 1990s, Friedrich's focus on subjectivity cuts across genres and breaks down absolute distinctions among them, typical for the "turn to the subject" in documentary film of the period (Renov, *Subject*, xi). The use of the "subjective camera shot" reflects the biographical perspective (MacDonald, "From Zygote" 31). The emphasis on the personal and subjective, especially in the underresearched genre of new queer documentary, transforms not only documentary's presumed reliance on objective facts but also, more important, encapsulates broad cultural shifts in response to marginalized voices that demand inclusion in national representations of history and culture (Geiger 178).

Friedrich's films of this period employ an ethnographic gaze on her upbringing and her family. She traces memories of queer and feminist subjects that invite recognition, identification, and reflection beyond individual experiences responding to filmmakers who in the 1970s began to engage in "domestic ethnography" as a response to the "crisis of ethnographic authority," a genre that examines autobiography (Renov, "Domestic Ethnography" 141). Thus, "the autobiographical 'self'" in

Friedrich's oeuvre functions as "a social subject" (Wees 33). Autobiography provides an entry into complex social relations, which include the nuclear family, fascism, and religion, among other issues.

The experimental mode lends itself to engaging memory because the intercutting of diverse threads and the disjunctive interaction of voice and image mimic memory's fragmentation, unreliability, and ambivalence. Evoking the process of remembering invites spectators to follow their own memories. The three films discussed in this section, *The Ties That Bind, Damned If You Don't*, and *Sink or Swim*, shatter taboos as they grapple with the charged memories of a German who grew up during the Nazi regime, sexual lesbian desire surrounding nuns, and the suppressed conflict with a famous and seemingly liberal father. Exploring and sharing emotions that are considered private reflect the feminist ethos to expose intimacy to an audience. The notion of the personal as political reframes memory and history and blends private and public.

Friedrich's subjective perspective embraces experimental cinema's ethos of choosing a peripheral status and imperfect aesthetics. Her emphasis on biography to address societal structures responds to feminism's valuation of the domestic space and the queer insistence on visibility in the public sphere. Friedrich eschews the fiction of universality that overdetermines mainstream cinema. Gunning consequently labels the experimental films of the late 1980s a "minor cinema." The phrase he adapted from Gilles Deleuze and Félix Guattari's volume *Kafka: Toward a Minor Literature* implies societal marginalization. These films "forswear aspiration to mastery" and celebrate "marginal identity, fashioning it from a revolutionary consciousness" ("Towards" 2). From this confluence of political and aesthetic movements, Friedrich molds a cinematic language to capture memories that fuse the Nazi past in Germany to American militarization and, in *Sink or Swim*, to engage critically with patriarchy by working through her relationship with her father.

Friedrich's three films interrogate visual records for their relationship to trauma for what queer-studies scholar Cvetkovich in the early twenty-first century calls "an archive of feelings," a shorthand with which she links trauma and sexuality to lesbian public cultures that national narratives rarely acknowledge (*Archive* 16). As trauma exerts pressure on familiar conventions of documentation and representation, it demands alternative forms of expression for collective witnessing that can contribute to new publics (Cvetkovich, *Archive* 16). Friedrich's films explore love, rage, intimacy, grief, and shame, which define queer life (Cvetkovich, *Archive* 7). Such memory culture responds to queerness in heterosexual family histories and energizes Friedrich's films. Friedrich's films rely on ephemeral, unorthodox, and suppressed materials to create queer and activist archives. The films render lesbian feelings visible in the process of constructing publics. Sharing memories fills the void left by the lack of institutional archives and documentation with the aim to transform official histories. In this way, the films open up spaces for contemplation on the specificity of lesbian desire and the inability of fixing that desire to one specific story (Mayne 208). Consequently, her films do not celebrate a particular lesbian identity but instead point to its multiple possibilities (Mayne 210).

The signifier "lesbian" in the wake of 1970s second-wave feminism and in relation to Friedrich's biography implies a political claim to feminist identity, while "queer" signals an anti-identitarian, deconstructive movement that emerged throughout the 1980s and 1990s. Yet, in recent years, scholars are rethinking the relation between these modes of identification. The term "queer" lacks the specificity of lesbian, while solely focusing on the latter does not account for the queer ways in which lesbians occupy that category (Cvetkovich, *Archive* 10–11). Friedrich's filmmaking mobilizes both the politics of lesbian feminism but also the strategies of queer deconstruction over the course of her career.

Friedrich's 1980s films advance an engagement with cinematic memory as part of a larger cultural transformation of public discourse, which develops into scholarly memory studies. Friedrich belongs to a group of several late twentieth-century feminist and lesbian filmmakers who mobilize the vernacular of memory to displace patriarchal hegemonic accounts of history. By excavating personal accounts of the past and contextualizing them within the present, the films point toward imagining a different kind of future. Scholar Jean Bessette calls this process "retroactivism," describing lesbian archives, in which activists curate the past for alternative politics in the present (2).[12] With the rise of memory studies, the theoretical notion of the archive expanded from an officially sanctioned collection in a specific geographic location with systematically organized and collected objects to a theory about a construction of collective memory (Halberstam, *In a Queer Time* 169–70). The transformation of the definition reflects collecting practices that, in turn, respond to political pressures and new technologies.

Friedrich's filmmaking invites feminist, female, lesbian, and queer spectatorship by expanding the tradition of experimental cinema, including the scratching of the film made famous by Brakhage and Mekas. Her haptic film language lends itself to capturing memories that reflect growing up female and queer. Two decades later, film scholars increase attention to what Laura U. Marks in her book of the eponymous title famously calls the "skin of the film" in relation to corporality (Vivian Sobchack), tactility (Jennifer M. Barker), and sensation (Martine Beugnet), all of which theorize the relationship among the senses, the body, and the screen. Marks explains "haptic visuality" as a way in which vision can be tactile by creating sensations of touch with one's eyes, which, she argues, characterizes feminist and experimental film and video of the period as they address perception, representations of sexuality, the senses, and embodiment (preface). Voice and its relation to the image may assume a particular function to activate cultural memories (preface). Friedrich often uses her own voice, which takes on a particularly emotional and biographical dimension. The voice-over ventriloquizes Friedrich's memories as well as those of other women, sharing intimate feelings with viewers. The scratched text increases the haptic dimension of her films.

These films imbricate intimate memories in public life. Later queer theory reframes the relationships among the personal and the public, the individual and the social, as they influence each other and take shape through the other (Ahmed, *Cultural* 14). Revisiting the feminist paradigm that the personal is political in the late 1990s, Lauren Berlant and Michael Warner famously reorient the discussion about private and public spheres by outlining how different publics mediate sex, including in "queer zones" (547). They emphasize imaginaries that arise from diverse forms of sexual and cultural identities that become intelligible in the public when the heterosexual couple no longer appears as the paradigm of sexual culture (548). In the United States, the family historically functioned as metaphor of the nation (549). Ideologies and institutions of intimacy relied on and reproduced assumptions of heterosexuality and limited futurity to generational reproduction (549–54).

In response, queer culture developed forms of intimacies that do not inherently relate to reproduction, family, kinship, and the nation and instead shape a counterpublic. Friedrich's exhibition practice extends this relationship to her audience.

Family Ties

The Ties That Bind, with a fifty-five-minute continuing interview between Friedrich and her German émigré mother Lore Bucher, launches the biographical turn in her oeuvre while continuing the experimental signature from her earlier films. In addition to translating memories into cinematic form, the film begins Friedrich's philosophical reflections on the nature of remembering, temporality, and the passing of time, investigating the function of memory for the relation of private and public history.

Throughout Friedrich's conversation with her mother, gender and sexuality define intergenerational relations and nationhood. Born 1920 in Ulm, Germany, Friedrich's mother immigrated to the United States after World War II with her American husband, who had been part of the US military occupational forces. The interview and the footage of Friedrich's own journey to Germany, which she documented with a Super 8 mm camera, "in a hand-held expressionist style reminiscent of Brakhage and Mekas" (MacDonald, "Su Friedrich: *The Ties*" 106), follow the subjective process of memory instead of paradigms of knowledge as is typical of documentary. Friedrich also recycles images, a technique that she embraces because she enjoys "finding new meanings, in a new context, for images that have appeared in earlier films" (MacDonald, "Damned" 7). Instead of chronological, cause-effect logic, the film unravels linear progressive time through memory that organizes its narrative. While emphasizing dialogic engagement, the film severs sound from image.

The Ties That Bind intercuts footage that Friedrich has shot for the film on her trip to Germany with handheld and gestural camerawork and archival films documenting burning German cities during World War II (MacDonald, "From Zygote" 30). Different sequences evoke private and public spheres from the past for the present. As the film advances in time, Lore's memories delve deeper into the past, reflecting the backward direction of the process of remembering. MacDonald contrasts the look of the Super 8 mm material that recalls home-movie travel diaries to the accounts of the mother's horrifying memories ("Su Friedrich: *The Ties*" 106).

The film situates the United States in a transnational context. It connects the story of Friedrich's mother growing up in Nazi Germany to the rise of anti-Semitism in the late twentieth century in the United States by showing letters from the Simon Wiesenthal Center and footage of Friedrich's participation and protest at the Women's Encampment for Peace and Justice. The visual track intersperses footage of Lore swimming with iconographies of popular culture, such as repeated images of marching bands in parades and pages of the *National Enquirer*. These materials contrast with footage of Friedrich visiting Lore's German hometown, Ulm, and the nearby Dachau concentration camp, as well as archival material of German cities being bombed during World War II.

Friedrich scratched questions for her mother into the celluloid to which Lore responds on the audio track. Manipulating the film strip serves a linguistic function integral to the dialogic structure of *The Ties That Bind*. Emphasizing the physicality of celluloid points to the material quality of memory. As Friedrich's mother answers the scratched questions extensively, Friedrich literally inscribes her signature into her film. The digital version maintains the original grainy quality and the flickering of projected celluloid. The daughter's silent questions and the mother's audible answers unmoor their relation from the convention of synchronous sound and image. The handwriting's intentional imperfection and the colloquial language foreground Friedrich's subjectivity in a material and affective way.[13] The questions diegetically address her mother and extradiegetically the spectators with the second person, "you." As the scratching emphasizes the filmic surface, it invites audience members to reflect on the medialization of memory. The hand-scratched questions appropriate the avant-garde practices of handworking the emulsion by Brakhage, Schneemann, and others (MacDonald, "Su Friedrich: *The Ties*" 105). Most important, haptic images invite viewers to respond in intimate, embodied ways (Marks 1). The fact that single words appear on each shot slows the process of reading. The questions carry their own weight instead of appearing solely as prompts for answers. Scott MacDonald points out, "Since viewers must construct the questions, one word at a time, they become, in a sense, *our* questions as well as

Friedrich's" ("Su Friedrich: *The Ties*" 105, emphasis in original). The writing interpellates the audience into the conversation.

Mother and daughter negotiate the past in a dialogic exchange about memory, which the mother shares and for which the daughter provides filmic images. The first scratched text, "When I was a kid, I never understood why my mother hated fireworks so much," instantiates the film's exploration of memory and history in a generational transfer (figure 7). The seemingly benign biographical observation focalizes the film's layers that include Friedrich's upbringing in the United States with a German mother after World War II, Lore's recollections of Nazi Germany, and Friedrich's journey to Germany. While the film interweaves mother's and daughter's memories, it also accounts for their previous inability to communicate about the impact of Lore's past on Friedrich's childhood. The filmmaker's experience of mediated memory and her attempt to use her film to overcome her lack of understanding her mother's past conjure up memory scholar Marianne Hirsch's concept of postmemory, which captures how a parent-survivor mediates the Holocaust for a child as "delayed, indirect, secondary" (13). Although Hirsch developed

Figure 7. Scratched text in
The Ties That Bind (1984)

her concept in relation to Holocaust survivors, Friedrich's film explores how secondary memory operates for those who belong to what scholar Michael Rothberg calls "the implicated subject," namely, those who occupy positions of privilege without being the direct agents of harm, such as her mother as a non-Jewish German (*Implicated* 1).

Friedrich homes in on the slippages among resistance, victimization, and empathy in the context of a German émigré's memory of the Nazi regime. Lore's story probes what German feminist scholar Christina Thürmer-Rohr had called *Mittäterschaft* (willing participation or participatory perpetratorship) when she demanded a feminist practice of working through the Nazi past—something that Friedrich is offering here. To engage in such a process collectively, the associative collage invites spectators to listen actively and to weigh and consider ambivalent and conflicting memories. The intercutting of footage from the Women's Encampment for Peace and Justice in the film's present tense and German burning cities during World War II bombing relates different historical moments and national locations to each other, implying the need for political action in the mid-1980s in a transnational feminist activist counterpublic.

The Ties That Bind reverses the assumption of photography as documentary evidence based on its indexicality on which postmemory relies. The film includes Lore gazing at photographs to emphasize the process of mediation instead of truth claims. Such a process of searching for echoes from the past differs from the notion of the photograph as witness and posits them instead as objects of negotiation. Friedrich questions what one gleans with certitude from visual documentations, infusing the film with a self-reflective dimension.

Denaturalizing the ideologies that undergird interrelated notions of family and the nation, the film maps what Ahmed calls "affective economies," which organize familial relations and lesbian desires (*Cultural* 46). The distinct audio and visual tracks sometimes reinforce, at other times confound the veracity of Lore's memories. Friedrich's process serves a crucial function in postmemory's collaborative narrative of parent and child, in which one provides the testimony while the other receives it (Hirsch 34). If dominant ideology obscures the political sphere by reducing it to familial relations, then Friedrich excavates the former from the latter and recontextualizes it to suggest historical continuities from the German past to the transnational rise of neo-Nazis and global militarization. Such associations also occur between seemingly incongruent features. For example, a hand draws a Hitler mustache onto a photograph of a young male model in an advertising page of an American magazine, which suggests a critique of surface culture of commodification and an inscription of Nazi iconography onto American popular culture.

The continuous intercutting of present and past, here and there, United States and Germany, and mother and daughter inscribes memory's multidirectionality and temporal layers. Friedrich translates the visual postmemory of the mother-daughter relationship into an archive for a feminist public sphere, in a process that Rothberg labels "multidirectional memory," which captures the relationship among different histories of victimization in the public sphere (*Multidirectional*). Friedrich depicts the present moment as fraught with the weight of the past and subjects her mother's memory to interactive negotiation. The filmmaker's prodding of her mother foregrounds the emotional labor involved in active remembering, such that the film locates both their efforts on a continuum of women's work across domestic and public arenas. Images of the *National Inquirer* with scraps from cleaning vegetables evoke women's domestic labor in the kitchen. The image of the newspaper located in the domestic sphere questions late twentieth-century theories about the formation of public life with the trace of female labor in the home, demolishing the rigid separation between the private and public spheres.

The film reminds us of the precarious situation of women between private and public as Lore's story oscillates between her personal experience and its larger historical significance, locating "the mother within *history*" (Fischer 194, emphasis in original). An investigation into German life under the Nazis cannot claim the private sphere as distinct from the public, and Friedrich exerts pressure on the leakages between those two areas. Connecting Lore's memory of the Nazi period to Friedrich's activism, the filmmaker offers visions of solidarity across time and place. Such an expanded understanding of history insists on the subjective and emotional dimensions of the political realm, making and remaking counterpublics through activist and artistic practices, including the creation of a feminist archive.

Cultural Memory and Lesbian Fantasy

Sandwiched between the two films about her parents is *Damned If You Don't* (1987), a film that expands personal remembrances into cultural memory and that creates an explicit lesbian narrative. It prepares Friedrich's turn to queer activism in the next decade. Actress and soprano Makea McDonald voices memories of seven women who had attended Catholic schools (see MacDonald, "Damned" 10). Her contributions accompany footage of contemporary nuns in Europe, a lesbian love story, and a deteriorated version of Michael Powell and Emeric Pressburger's classic 1947 British film *Black Narcissus* running on a television set within the diegesis. *Damned If You Don't* creates a collective fantasy of lesbian desire, stitching together Northern Italian medieval history of a nun accused of indecent behavior and a story of a contemporary female artist and a nun that culminates in their sexual encounter.

Friedrich mines the classic film for its melodramatic and erotic potential. Her own film adds another dimension to the 35 mm technicolor *Black Narcissus*, which adapted author Rumer Godden's best-selling novel from 1939 about a group of British nuns in an isolated cloister in the Himalayas. Godden had lived in England and India as the daughter of a steamer agent (Street 3). According to some scholars, the novel depicts the decline of the British Empire (Street 7). Others accused it of advancing "imperialist fantasies," which Friedrich excises (Holmlund, "Feminist" 225). Queer filmmakers repeatedly turn to the genre of melodrama, since it offers a site "for cinematic investigations of the connections and disjunctures among sex, gender, and desire," which it conventionally inscribes as heterosexual (Holmlund, "Feminist" 224). *Damned If You Don't* recontextualizes the canonical melodramatic text to mobilize its lesbian potential.

Damned If You Don't appropriates *Black Narcissus* by rewriting and queering the character constellation. The artist, played by performance artist, actress, and director Ela Troyano, also called Other Woman, whom Holmlund reads as "the (Latina) girl" encounters and falls in love with a nun, played by Peggy Healey ("Feminist" 224). The two main characters echo and revise the figures of the Good Nun and the Bad Nun from *Black Narcissus*, whom film-studies scholar Chris Straayer interprets as "one saintly, the other sexual" and who form an erotic, repressed triangle with one of the film's few male characters, Mr.

Dean (211). Straayer explains, "Mr. Dean, of course, desires the pure woman but honors the religious vocation," while the sexual advances of the Bad Nun only increase his desire for the good one (211). Friedrich excavates the film's submerged erotic energy and claims it for a lesbian love story.

Damned If You Don't reinterprets and recuperates existing marginalized and repressed cultural archives to assert lesbian desire in public. Subjective memories coalesce to a shared experience of being raised or educated by nuns that differs from either the idealized or the sexualized perception of them. The audio of disembodied memories conjuring up emotions from the past and projecting them into the present infuses what appears on the screen. The voice-over anchors the film in the collective biographical experiences of women who came of age in the late 1950s, developed into feminists, and came out as lesbians in the 1970s. More than her previous work and preparing the ground for her explicitly political documentaries, this film advances a lesbian narrative, which culminates in a sex scene. The subtle accounts of growing up foreshadows Friedrich's later work on lesbian childhood in Hide and Seek. Memories, ephemeral by nature, make up the queer archive.

Nuns

The role of Catholicism for the repression and expression of sexuality in the maturation process of girls reoccurs throughout Friedrich's work, from the earlier Gently Down the Stream to the later Hide and Seek. Damned If You Don't explores the nonconformity of nuns in the ideology of heterosexual reproduction. The film appeared three years after the translation of Michel Foucault's History of Sexuality into English, which turned the repression theory, inherited from Sigmund Freud, on its head. Foucault explained that not only did religion repress sexuality but that it also produced discourse about it. Intriguingly, the voice-over describes exactly that process by telling stories of nuns whose instructions and warnings about desire created sexual curiosity. These intimate memories about nuns as teachers convey deep and lasting attachments. By conjoining personal remembrances with images that are loosely related but not literal illustrations of the anecdotes, the film emphasizes associative connections, typical of the process of remembering.

Sound and image derive from different sources and reference diverse genres. The film includes footage that Friedrich shot of nuns, for example in Venice, Italy, where she traveled during an artist residency in West Berlin with the German Academic Exchange Service. These images of nuns in the public interweave with the narrative about the female artist and the nun. The two characters encounter each other in public spaces until the very end when they return to the artist's apartment. Quinlan reads excerpts from historian Judith C. Brown's 1986 scholarly book *Immodest Acts: The Life of a Lesbian Nun* in a voice-over that accompanies the visual track.

Lesbian history serves as intertext for the multiple layers of intermediality. Brown, a scholar of early modern Italy, relates the story of Sister Benedetta Carlini of Vellano, born in 1590 and later abbess of the Theatine nuns of Pescia, who became the object of ecclesiastical investigations in the mid-seventeenth century. The Renaissance imaginary of celestial gardens and interior and exterior landscapes of cemeteries, churches, and cloisters defines *Damned If You Don't*'s mise-en-scène. With the repeated shots of the outdoor enclosures in different seasons, Friedrich pays homage to the garden as symbol of the Virgin Mary (Brown 48). Benedetta Carlini experienced terrifying visions, such that her superiors assigned her a companion, Bartolomea Crivelli. An investigation following Bartolomea Crivelli's claim that Benedetta persuaded her to "engage in the most immodest acts" concluded that the devil seduced Benedetta (Brown 117). Brown emphasizes that "two women should seek sexual gratification with each other was virtually inconceivable" and that, therefore, Benedetta assumes a male identity as an angel (118). The film's voice-over quotes Brown's explicit description as Bartolomea relates that Benedetta grabbed her "hand by force, and putting it under herself, she would have her put her finger into her genitals and holding it there she stirred herself so much that she corrupted herself" (120). Subsequently, Benedetta spent thirty-five years in prison.

Reworking Melodrama

The film's diverse footage appropriates existing imagery for a transgressive vision. As with her other films, Friedrich begins *Damned If You Don't* without an establishing shot or a narrative exposition. In the opening footage, a relaxed nun strides down a busy street while eating ice cream. Heads of passersby interrupt the spectator's view of her. The subsequent close-up of lighting a candle evokes a religious symbol, only to reveal a room with a mattress, a small television set on the floor, and an aquarium—the minimalist domestic setting of the main character. The mise-en-scène signals the onset of a narrative. A young woman reclines on her bed and watches *Black Narcissus* on her television with roll bars on its screen. When grainy sequences from the old film fill the screen of *Damned If You Don't*, a typescript announces the location "Convent of the Order of the Servants of Mary—Calcutta" over an image of a nun staring out a large window. Martina Siebert's voice-over recounts the plot of *Black Narcissus* in a bare-bone summary with a "humorous delivery" that "brings out the melodrama and 'hysteria'" (Street 78). In the close-ups of the downgraded copy of the original technicolor film, the nuns' habits frame their faces and highlight their eyes, while the high-contrast shadows endow the setting with a noirish quality, and the bodies in their tunics create geometric compositions. Friedrich decontextualizes moments from the narrative, for example, when nuns surround Mr. Dean, who appears bare-chested, clad only in shorts and a hat. As the film's emphasis on the nuns' cloaks renders their physical contours of the female form abstract, the shot's composition evokes a circuit of desire that reverses the typical gendering of visual representation.

The intercutting of *Black Narcissus*, which also diegetically plays on television, the story of the female artist and the young nun she encounters in the street, and the footage that Friedrich herself shot relate the different sources to each other. When the unnamed artist hangs a canvas behind her bed and paints it, its landscape echoes *Black Narcissus's* production in the Pinewood Studios outside of London where German émigré designer Alfred Junge drew the artificial set (Street 17).[14] The crosscuts between the artist and the nun in their everyday activities creates an expectation for a romantic encounter, invoking traditional editing to anticipate a meeting between two main characters. Holmlund points out that "all the desiring that occurs in the constant shot/reverse shots, point-of-view shot and eyeline matches takes place between women" ("Feminist" 228–29). A shaky camera in the street, for example, from the point of view of the artist following the nun into a church, captures the simultaneous visibility of the characters and the invisibility of their desire in the public space.

Experimental editing interweaves medieval paintings and historical documentation of the life of nuns with present-day lesbian desire. The excerpt from Giovanni di Paolo's painting *The Last Judgement, Detail of the Predella Panel Depicting Paradise* (ca. 1460–1465) of two medieval nuns holding each other reappears throughout the film. Over footage of contemporary nuns walking alone or together in the streets, the voice-over recites the testimony of Sister Bartolomea, who was to accompany Sister Benedetta and had a sexual relationship with her, only to denounce her later. While the artist reads Brown's book in a garden, the voice-over recounts Sister Bartolomea's testimony of how Jesus removed the heart of Sister Benedetta. Embodying the archival documents through a living voice forges a connection across time and media. Similarly, after the nun and the artist encounter each other in a store, match cuts between the contemporary nun opening a door and a clip of *Black Narcissus* with a point-of-view shot of a character entering the exotic space of the film create the illusion of merging past and present. Friedrich continuously intercuts two stories in different temporal planes, for example, one of the nuns in *Black Narcissus* dramatically ringing the bells while she and another nun are attempting to push each other into the bell tower's abyss, and another of the encounter between the nun and the artist in a contemporary city. Through the editing, each narrative vignette inflects the other.

Lesbian Lovemaking and Scandalous Nuns

The film concludes with an explicit lesbian sex scene. Its silent nature enhances the aesthetics of the eroticism. In the film's final scene, the nun visits the artist. Adorned in sensual clothes, the artist slowly undresses the nameless and silent nun, revealing her body beneath the heavy cloth. As the episode of the entanglement of the nude bodies concludes the stories and remembrances of disavowed sexuality, the film revises the existing archive of marginalized desires for future possibilities of lesbian attraction and sociability. The physical presence of the bodies for an audience to witness contrasts with the film's emphasis on fantasy and claims realness for lesbian desire. Framing the nun as an object of lesbian fantasy reflects a submerged understanding of the figure as a symbol of an alternative lifestyle under heterosexual patriarchy.

When the film concludes with the lesbian love-making scene, it releases the built-up tension in their final erotic encounter, which gains a privileged status because no other visual or verbal material interrupts the sequence. The simple plot relies on an archetypal formula: two strangers meet and fall in love, which the film propels forward with classic crosscutting. Neither the main character nor the nun speaks; instead, they use gestural language. Friedrich aligns the camera with the imaginary point of view of the main character as the film repeatedly follows nuns in cities, instantiating a voyeuristic gaze with distant shots, often from behind or in crowds. The intense sensuality and intimacy of the final scene extend to the spectators. *Damned If You Don't* moves from rereading and remediating Renaissance Italy and postwar cinema to the assertion of lesbian existence through the explicit sex act, doubling the claim to lesbian authorship and agency.

Depictions of nuns command an interest for a male heterosexual imagination about sex because they, like lesbians, live in a homosocial environment, independent from men. Nuns and lesbians are in instances mistaken for each other because they are oblivious to male attention and because they eschew conventional femininity (Curb 401). In the 1970s their status as objects of male sexual fantasies fueled a wave of nunsploitation films that sometimes combined sex with horror. Nuns' status as virginal paradoxically allows for projections of sexual fantasies. Exploitation films associated nuns with perversion, including lesbianism, sexualizing them in a subculture. Experimental cinema is a far cry politically or narratively from the conventions of exploitation cinema, yet B movies share with the avant-garde that they both break taboos and differ from the high production value of Hollywood film. Cross-pollination between academic feminism and underground film festivals also connects avant-garde cinema and sexploitation film. Feminist experimental filmmakers Ahwesh and M. M. Serra, for example, championed Doris Wishman, one of the very few women working as director and producer in the sexploitation industry (Gorfinkel 437). Especially powerful in Catholic countries, such as Poland, Italy, France, and Portugal but also the United States and Japan, nun exploitation films include, among others, *Our Lady of Lust* (Sergio Bergonzelli, Italy, 1972), *School of the Holy Beast* (Seiju Gakuen, Japan, 1974), and *The Sinful Nuns of Saint Valentine* (Sergio Grieco, Italy, 1974). Lesbian sex scenes are as "obligatory in nun movies" as the genre's key image "of a nun naked except for her white headpiece" (Fujiwara n.p.).

Friedrich participates in transvaluing the existing archive of nunsploitation and midcentury melodrama to avant-garde film for lesbian romance, desire, and sexuality. In the history of nonnormative desires, sexploitation films played a significant role for gays and lesbians, offering rare opportunities to see representations of themselves, even if hyperbolically inaccurate. Sexploitation film emerged in the 1960s as a precursor to pornography in the 1970s (Gorfinkel 87). From roughly 1960 to 1970, hundreds of sexploitation films featured perversion and sexual deviance, as well as nonnormative sexual practices and emergent identities, such as lesbianism (see Gorfinkel). Elena Gorfinkel situates those representations in the changing public life of the 1960s, which included the women's movement and the emergence of gay liberation politics (179). Sexploitation does not show explicit sex acts. Those occur off-screen, in stark contrast to the explicit final love-making scene on screen in *Damned If You Don't*.

The 1970s political imperative to come out of the closet not only transformed film culture with a rallying call to disavow subtexts and, instead, embrace a coherent positive identity. It also affected the public image of nuns who embraced their lesbian desire and identity, most famously with the 1985 publication of *Lesbian Nuns: Breaking Silence*, edited by Nancy Manahan and Rosemary Keefe Curb. Coeditors Curb and Manahan met at the 1981 National Women's Studies Association Conference, and Naiad Press publisher Barbara Grier advanced a contract because she recognized the book's financial potential. The collection broke silence around lesbians in convents as conditions for nuns began to change after Vatican II and with the rise of feminism (Passet 133). Yet, controversy surrounded the book, on the one hand, between mainstream Catholicism and feminist nuns and, on the other hand, between academic feminists and lesbians of an earlier generation.

Grier belonged to the generation of lesbians that had come out in the 1940s prior to the feminist or gay and lesbian liberation movements, different than the editors and contributors who belonged to the generation of the 1970s second-wave feminist lesbians. She advertised the anthology as "explosive" and "controversial" to television talk shows and radio stations without informing the two editors, who, along with their contributors, had envisioned a small lesbian and academic readership. Instead, conservative audiences on talk shows harassed the editors with hostile questions, and Catholic leadership denounced the book as "sensational" and "bizarre" (Passet 183). An internal conflict erupted between Naiad Press and the editors and contributors. When the publishing house sold excerpts to a softcore pornographic magazine published by Bob Guccione's Penthouse Ltd., the gay and lesbian community became outraged with Grier for projecting pornographic sexualization onto women who excised themselves from heterosexual relations for a spiritual life. Such background provides a context for the interest in nuns as part of the feminist movement and lesbian communities at the time of the film's making.

Simultaneously, *Damned If You Don't* also belongs to a wave of queer cinema in the mid-1980s that recuperated subtexts of mainstream films for a vision of lesbian spectatorship. Like many of these films, *Damned If You Don't* interpellates spectators into the lesbian subject-positions of viewing, beginning with the artist watching *Black Narcissus* in the film's opening scene. Those films were key for the theorization of cinema's role in queer desire. Holmlund wonders about experimental films' embrace of recycling sounds, images, and story lines from earlier movies ("Feminist" 217). She explains, in her analysis of Friedrich's *Damned If You Don't*, that this practice undermines essential definitions of gender, sexuality, or race ("Feminist" 218). Key films from the period, similarly, recut classic films. For example, Cecilia Barriga's *Meeting of Two Queens* (1991) combines different films starring Marlene Dietrich and Greta Garbo to imagine a lesbian love story between the two women, while Mark Rappaport's *Rock Hudson's Home Movies* (1992) includes scenes from Rock Hudson's films to excavate their homosexual subtext. Sheila McLaughlin's *She Must Be Seeing Things* (1987) tells the story of a lesbian couple that edits a film about Catalina, a seventeenth-century rebellious woman, which led film scholar Teresa de Lauretis to herald the film as "rearticulating the function of voyeurism both diegetically and cinematically" (228). These films unearth subtextual queer readings from classic texts with an emphasis on identification and projection. *Damned If You Don't* explores the different ways in which fantasies circulate in public and private spaces through characters on screen who function in mediating roles for spectators.

Like the other films in this section, *Damned If You Don't*'s editing of the image track and soundtrack triggers audience members' own memories and invites reflection on connections across differing materials, historical moments, and geographic locations (figure 8). Yet, different than *Ties that Bind* and the later *Sink or Swim, Damned If You Don't* adds a barebone narrative to the experimental style that Friedrich established in her previous films. Through intercutting, the different source texts collide to address spectators affectively, like Friedrich's *Gently Down the Stream*'s invocation of dreams. Similar to the process in *Scar Tissue*, the repeated observational shots of nuns in Venice train the eye to see them anew, as subjects with agency and passion. The film contributes to an archive of lesbian desire.

Patriarchal Pedagogy

Friedrich's 1990 film *Sink or Swim* appears as a companion piece to *The Ties That Bind*, as she turns again to her birth family, focusing on

Figure 8. Poster for Friedrich retrospective in Frankfurt, Germany (2019), originally in color. Image courtesy Su Friedrich

her father, Paul Wilhelm Friedrich. By the time Friedrich made *Sink or Swim*, she was an established experimental filmmaker. Five years after *Ties That Bind* and three years after *Damned If You Don't*, *Sink or Swim* shares with the two other films the assemblage of different source materials, written text, and voice-over. Taken together, these films highlight association as the core mechanism for probing the productivity of memories to address historical guilt, forbidden desire, and the figure of the modern patriarch. While the films about her parents seem to offer a solely private archive, the emotional world that they evoke speaks to the subtle devaluing of women as mothers and daughters. Her father emerges as publicly sensitive but privately selfish, who narcissistically projects oedipal desire onto his daughter.

In *Sink or Swim* Friedrich remembers her relationship to linguist, anthropologist, and poet Paul Wilhelm Friedrich (1927–2016), professor of social thought at the University of Chicago. After Friedrich's parents met in Germany and moved to the United States in the 1950s, Paul Friedrich completed research in Mexico accompanied by her mother and her sister, Maria. With a 1957 PhD from Yale University, he became an influential scholar, first at the University of Pennsylvania and later at the University of Chicago. After he left Su Friedrich's family, he remarried twice.

The 48-minute black-and-white film follows the reverse order of the alphabet. It consists of twenty-six vignettes by Friedrich about her father, which Jessica Meyerson as a young girl recounts in a voice-over, a "Friedrich surrogate," who shares memory fragments (Renov, "Domestic Ethnography" 143). A single word in white typescript on black background begins with a letter of the alphabet in succession, from "Zygote" to the three Greek goddesses "Athena, Atalanta, and Aphrodite." Neither does the spoken text directly explicate the image track, nor does each keyword consistently identify or announce the images that follow. The film undermines linearity through "thematic discontinuities among the lexia as well as by the frequently oblique character of the sound/image relations," which follow the "dream logic of recovered memory" (Renov, "Domestic Ethnography" 143). Image and soundtracks relate to each other in open-ended, diverse ways, summoning further associations by the audience. Its "wide range of visual material" creates an "intricate network of connections between sound and image" (MacDonald, "From

Zygote" 32). Such strategies constantly call upon spectators to engage in emotional responses instead of cognitive comprehension.

The overarching principle of associative combination mimics the working of memory and invites audience members to conjure up their own familial pasts. The film includes material that Friedrich shot herself, as well as home movies. These materials are often not immediately distinguishable from each other. In instances, the visuals are reminiscent of memories of Friedrich's childhood. Sources include a range of registers from scientific films to Friedrich's material, for example, of female bodybuilders. The first episode, "Zygote," includes a sperm impregnating an egg, initiating an origin story. A later chapter, "Memory," recounts the tragic and dramatic death of her father's sister as a teenager over a scene from a grainy home movie that her grandfather shot with her father as a young boy with his sister. For the section "Flesh," Friedrich shot footage to accompany the story of a trip to Mexico to which her father invited her when she was young, only to send her back early, and "Bigamy" depicts the adult Friedrich smoking, drinking, and watching television. Through the course of the episodes, the film reveals her father's narcissistic personality, the director's relationship with him, and the impact of her parents' breakup. Thus, while the formal structure appears paratactic, and the linguistic organization reverses the familiar order, the film chronicles the intimate process of Friedrich's disappointment with and liberation from her father.

The downgraded quality of the opening biological education film about the sperm impregnating an egg signals an earlier era, coinciding with Friedrich's own schooling. By the late 1980s, organizations and schools no longer projected film for instructional and informational purposes. From the 1950s to the 1970s, however, it was a common experience to enter a classroom with the lights being switched off while the "16mm projector whirrs, triggering a beam of light leading to a screen in the front of the room" (Orgeron, Orgeron, and Streible 3). Instruction via projected film was the norm around the world in classrooms, libraries, public meeting rooms, and museums. Yet, the act of gathering to watch educational film was already outdated at the time of *Sink or Swim*'s making. Institutions had shifted to video as a tool for illustrating knowledge and imparting information. The sequence's grainy quality gestures to an archive of disappeared viewing practices.

Relatedly, home movies spawn nostalgia. Because they are inherently about the past, they appear with the grainy quality of celluloid in feature narrative films or documentaries to signify gone-by days. When repurposed, they signal nostalgia with the aesthetics of a handheld shaky camera, faded colors, grainy quality, and scenes of domestic and familial bliss. In *Sink or Swim*, the child's voice recuperates the past in the present and resurrects the accompanying emotions.

Through the course of *Sink or Swim*, Friedrich deconstructs the presumed objectivity of knowledge as she unravels how her father's scholarship and poetry conflict with his private behaviors. She appropriates and creatively refunctionalizes scientific discourses to question their veracity. Knowledge emerges as a vehicle of power that her father wields with his public success born out of white male heterosexual privilege going hand in glove with his selfishness. *Sink or Swim* invokes a broader cultural context by including pop cultural celebrations of patriarchs with footage from 1950s television shows, such as *Make Room for Daddy* and *Father Knows Best*.

Sink or Swim questions the validity of images from both private and public spheres. The film's experimental multimedia captures the complexity of subjective memory in relation to archival traces. Images do not illustrate events that the voice-over recounts. The narrator, for example, describes the girl's birthday party when she went to the ice rink with her friends, who enjoyed skating with her father. When she skated with him, his speed was so fast that she could not keep up. Responding to the accompanying footage that Friedrich shot for the film, a viewer struggles with the question of reliability, trying to decipher the images in relation to the narrated biographical memories. Is the young girl Su Friedrich? Does this matter?

The film calls upon spectators to negotiate the unreliability of memory vis-à-vis what Alison Landsberg calls its "prosthesis," most often filmic images that substitute for memories. Similarly, the narrator relays the story of the father's traumatic loss of his teenaged sister, who suffered a heart attack after she jumped into a swimming pool with ice-cold water. Grainy images of a young boy and a young girl on a path and footage of a pool depict her father and his sister at a young age. This excerpt of a home movie in which we see degraded images of two teenagers in the past walking down a street is unable to capture the subjective experience of Friedrich's father's trauma when he was a child. The emotional register of the home movie does not capture the horrific event. Instead, viewers confront the gap of signification that remains throughout the film and inheres in family photos and visual documentation, in general.

Sink or Swim continues the inquiry into memory and visual documentation that Friedrich began with *The Ties That Bind*, as both probe the visual family archive as a "site of conflicting memories" (Kuhn 14). *Sink or Swim* asks viewers to search the existing footage for traces of trauma, neglect, and lack of care, rendering visible the expectation for home movies and family photos to document the idealized family for its members to gain future access to what then will be the past. Friedrich's film thus questions home movies' claims to authenticity. In the material that she shot for this film, the director explores conflicting accounts of familial pasts. Tensions, contradictions, and incongruencies that emerge from the contrasting remembrances exceed the indexical quality of the image.

Sink or Swim's episodes, mimicking the way in which memory operates, chart the emotions of a girl confronting her father's power. Through the course of the film, Friedrich develops a psychological profile of upper-middle-class and white masculinity. MacDonald suggests that the film captures "the brutality built into the conventional nuclear family by virtue of societal gender assumptions" ("Daddy" 28). Instead of using violence or force, the father actively dismisses Friedrich. The turning point occurs late in the film, when the narrator witnesses her father displaying his lack of attention vis-à-vis a story that her much-younger stepsister begins to tell. She remembers a meeting with her father and his younger daughter and recounts how he explicitly expresses his disinterest in her story, which reminds Friedrich of her own experiences as a child. Seeing the scene played out in front of her enables her to gain insight and mastery of her understanding of her father. The filmmaker can only articulate the intimate emotions of hope, pain, and disappointment in hindsight from the vantage point of an adult.

The film's centerpiece thematizes the broad cultural significance of her mother's experience of loss. It works through Lore mourning the departure of her husband, which the director unravels in different episodes that build on each other around the leitmotif of German composer Franz Schubert's 1814 song "Gretchen at the Spinning Wheel,"

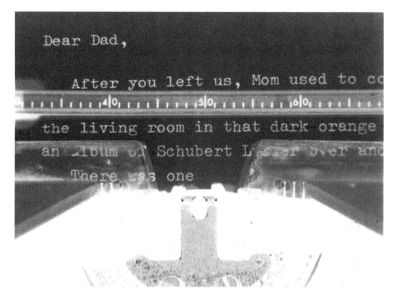

Figure 9. Letter to the father in *Sink or Swim*
(1990). Image courtesy Su Friedrich

beginning in the section "Kinship." Midway through the film, this episode consists of different contrasting images, including desert landscapes
and women making out in a shower, all the while that the song "Gretchen
at the Spinning Wheel" accompanies the entire length of the episode.
In a later section, "Ghosts," a close-up on negative film centers on a
typewriter, at which Friedrich is writing a letter to her father, revealing
that after he left the family, her mother sent the children to their rooms
and played Schubert's song repeatedly while sitting in the dark (figure 9).

The biographical narrative of the mother's despair and the text of
the song reflect the trauma inflicted on women in intimate relations
with powerful men. The narrator addresses the absent father in a voice-
over telling a story that when the mother cried listening to this song,
the children would come out and promise her to be good so that their
father would return. An audience knows that the children are neither
responsible for the father's action nor for their mother's anguish and
that they cannot undo her despair. The song's text, which Friedrich's
mother would have known well, is the famous monologue by the female

character Gretchen in Johann Wolfgang von Goethe's 1808 classic drama *Faust: A Tragedy*. In the drama, the main character of the eponymous name, the brilliant scholar Dr. Faust, aims to overcome his human limitation to gain knowledge in science by making a pact with the devil. He seduces Gretchen, and her melodramatic monologue occurs when she contemplates suicide because she is alone, unwed, and pregnant. The drama presents a paradigm of male knowledge and female physicality, as Faust impregnated Gretchen, the female vessel bound to and limited by her childbearing.

The melancholic song presents a blueprint of male freedom to achieve greatness unfettered by familial responsibilities, in contrast to women limited by their reproductive function. Schubert's song captures Gretchen's spinning activity musically by expressing her heartache in D minor, with the instrumental accompaniment of the right hand mimicking the perpetual movement of the spinning wheel and the left hand imitating the foot treadle. The mother listens to the record turning repeatedly, like Gretchen's spinning wheel. The image of Lore sitting in the dark with the disk rotating echoes the circular movement of the spinning wheel in the drama's original scene. Similarly, Friedrich's mother's threat to kill herself and her children after her ex-husband's visit invokes Gretchen's infanticide that occurs late in the classic play.

Revisiting the Oedipal Drama

Sink or Swim rewrites Freud's foundational understanding of the oedipal drama as shaping family dynamics as a father's projection onto his daughter. The memory that defines the relation between Friedrich and her father occurs in the episode "Flesh" and reverberates throughout the subsequent final four episodes. When her father takes her as a young teenager on a trip to Mexico, she misses lunch and dinner, and he sends her back alone on a plane. In the following section, "Envy," she finds a later poem he wrote about the incident, which accuses her of having found Adonis on the beach. Friedrich, the filmmaker, in the present retorts that he had been acting like a scorned and vengeful lover and exposes the oedipal narrative as a male projection onto a daughter. In the next section, "Discovery," she applies an anthropological model about the kinship system to his three marriages, turning his own master discourse against him and subverting presumed scholarly neutrality that allowed him to exclude personal accountability (figures 10 and 11). By reversing the alphabet and mimicking the mapping of kinship, Friedrich appropriates her father's disciplines, linguistics and anthropology, to expose the personal price his families and daughters paid for his public success.

The use of the alphabet illuminates the systemic structures beyond Friedrich's autobiography. The film concludes in the present tense when in the penultimate story, "Bigamy," a grown Friedrich watches television while the voice-over recounts how she spent a day with her father and his daughter of his third marriage. The appearance of the film's director in the diegesis doubles her in front and behind the camera. The film's final episode concludes with Friedrich swimming in a lake, jettisoning her father's haunting presence. She uses the alphabet, his domain as a linguist, to overcome his dominance, mining her biography but transcending the limitation of her individual experience.

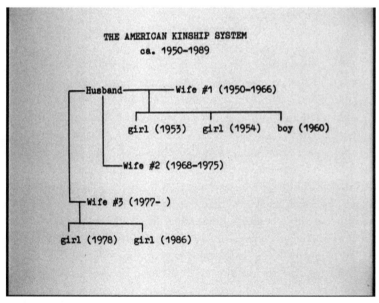

Figure 10. Kinship model of Friedrich's family
in *Sink or Swim* (1990)

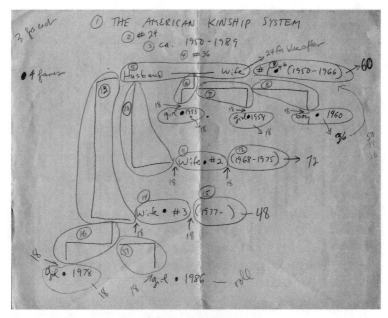

Figure 11. Friedrich mapping out the kinship
model of her family for *Sink or Swim* (1990).
Image courtesy Su Friedrich

Over the course of these three films, Friedrich develops a visual
language of memory that reflects lesbian feminist sensibility. Taken
together, *The Ties That Bind, Damned If You Don't,* and *Sink or Swim*
provide a window into a life of a daughter of a German immigrant
to the United States after World War II, lesbians who were educated
by nuns, and a girl who was abandoned by her father. The films offer
insight into a generation that came into consciousness on the heels
of the political liberation movements of the 1970s. The films engage
affectively, emotionally, and theoretically with the working of memory
and its fragmented nature. In addition, the films explore the ways to
mine individual and collective memories to imagine a different future.
Friedrich captures the backward glance of remembering by shooting
material that appears like films from the past. The later scholarly turn
to archive, memory, and emotion as cultural practices and integral to
counterpublics, especially for marginalized queer subjects and their
lives, theorizes what Friedrich captures artistically. By unearthing the

patriarchal family structures that allowed her father to abandon her family and enjoy public success, Friedrich visualizes the feminist slogan "the personal is political."

Friedrich shooting material of the past either in a documentary or metaphorical mode illustrates what film studies scholar Jaimie Baron calls "the archive effect." She argues that historically archives have been official holding places for film. As online databases with amateur photography, film, and video have proliferated, the distinction between archival and found materials has deteriorated, but shots that appear as if produced at diverse moments in time inscribe into the text a difference between then and now (Baron 103–6). *Sink or Swim* stages for spectators the presence of that past through archival traces, which simultaneously always point to the absence of what has been lost (Baron 109).

Friedrich expands the archive affect as images and sounds from the past derive from different registers, including sound recordings, home movies, metaphorical commentary, and reenactments, inviting spectators to engage emotionally and cognitively with the question of the veracity of both filmic material and memories. When audiences ask, for example, whether the little girl on the ice rink is really the young Friedrich or an actress, they are reflecting not only on questions about the indexicality of the image but also on the human ability to access the past accurately. Friedrich's oeuvre offers the pleasure of watching beautiful films that challenge spectators to ponder cinema's evidentiary nature.

The films grouped together here, therefore, also offer a form of media archeology, an investigation of what happens when an experimental filmmaker edits together British studio films, home movies, archival footage of a burning German city, her own footage of nuns in Venice, political activism, and scenes of lesbian lovemaking. Such films challenge spectators to think and feel beyond the visible and to follow the yellow brick road of poetic riddles to make sense of their own realities and their own pasts.

The Politics of Being Lesbian

During the 1990s Friedrich asserts lesbian specificity in an increasingly political cinema while continuing her signature stylistic features. Avant-garde aesthetics and radical lesbian politics reinforce each other and define her films for a decade when activists appropriate the term "queer" to deconstruct the notion of clearly circumscribed sexual identities and to name the plurality of nonnormative desires. When the culture wars embroiled right-wing politicians and gay and lesbian artists, filmmaking became part of the activist toolbox. Within her repertoire, Friedrich continues to highlight how the repetition of gestures produces gender, how its normative articulation supports heterosexual institutions, and how memory provides access to the past experiences by marginalized subjects.

Over the course of her career, Friedrich demonstrates that the two modalities of experimental cinema and activist documentary reinforce each other. Experimental practices, such as cutting and editing for cadences, scratching celluloid, and relating script, image, and sound as independent but intersecting planes, remain characteristic of her filmmaking. The editing that featured prominently in her early titles, specifically *Scar Tissue* and *But No One*, continues to define her films during the 1990s, such as *First Comes Love* (1991), *Rules of the Road* (1993), and *Hide and Seek* (1996), although she embraces a documentary style in her collaboration with Janet Baus on *Lesbian Avengers Eat Fire, Too* (1993). In the last decade of the twentieth century, Friedrich reaches audiences beyond aficionados of experimental cinema and receives significant funding and awards.

Friedrich's form of auteurism includes political, aesthetic, and personal investment in forms of mutual support, exchange, cooperation, and collaboration. Shared "participation, consensus, and working toward common goals" shape her films in the form of coauthored scripts, codirected films, and contributions by friends (*Camera Obscura* Collective, "Collectivity: Part 1," 1). Her work maintains the tradition of feminist and queer filmmakers who have engaged in collective practices since the 1960s as part of a "larger aesthetic and political program" (Columpar 6). Beginning with her early film *Cool Hands, Warm Heart*, Friedrich cooperates with others on- and off-screen to the extent that an ethos of mutual support and exchange defines her authorship and aesthetics. For example, *Lesbian Avengers Eat Fire, Too* and *Hide and Seek* limit the shot–reverse shot, which traditionally highlights relations among individual characters (Murray 101). Her commitment to cooperative practices persists throughout her career, even after "the era of feminist video collectives" waned when the feminist movement entered the mainstream in the 1980s and after cheaper video cameras provided access to technology (Bociurkiw 21). Feminist film scholars have questioned whether an emphasis on cooperation cedes ground to the celebration of the singular male auteur, and Friedrich serves as an important example of an artist who integrates joint efforts into her filmmaking practice that is, however, singularly recognizable and carries an auteurist signature (see Columpar 6–7). Her continuous emphasis on collaboration connects feminist to queer filmmaking in ways that histories of the two movements tend to overlook.

During the 1990s Friedrich's four films explore the politics of queer intimacy, observing rituals of heterosexual institutions that denounce lesbian existence. Her twenty-two-minute, 16 mm, silent film *First Comes Love* tethers together the implied critique of the heterosexual wedding ritual with a statement about the impossibility of lesbian and gay marriage. Two years later, Friedrich codirects with Baus the sixty-minute documentary about the Lesbian Avengers, *Lesbian Avengers Eat Fire, Too*. Her thirty-one-minute, color film *Rules of the Road*, of the same year, centers on station wagons as objects that represent the collapse of her lesbian relationship. This cluster of films concludes in 1996 with the financially well-supported and critically recognized one-hour-and-five-minute, black-and-white film *Hide and Seek*. The film intercuts a narrative, interviews, and segments of educational films, grappling with the possibility of a lesbian childhood. It shares with the earlier *Damned If You Don't* the evocation of memories and reflects on lesbian identity through collective voices. Once Friedrich's work focuses on the specificity of lesbian identity, it becomes programmed as lesbian at festivals, and individual scholars warn of the danger of essentializing the films (Holmlund, "When Autobiography" 139–40).

Friedrich accompanies the representation of lesbian politics with an increased interest in the documentary mode. This situates her at the periphery of the purview of feminist film studies, because in the 1970s those scholars neglected documentary filmmaking practice. When feminist film activism developed into an academic field, its attention shifted from realist documentary to privileging avantgarde and experimental film (Juhasz 179; see also Rich, *Chick Flicks*). Following feminist-film scholar Mulvey's foundational article, "Visual Pleasure and Narrative Cinema," which defines feminist-film theory as the psychoanalytic critique of Hollywood cinema, the field marginalized the documentary tradition and privileged antirealism. Feminist-film theory focused on a theoretical critique of dominant narrative cinema, thereby sidelining documentary film and its makers (Waldman and Walker 7–8). Feminist and documentary film studies in the 1970s radically diverged. Documentary studies ignored feminist perspectives, even though the women's movement embraced documentary filmmaking because of cheap and accessible 16 mm film and video equipment, a practice that scholarship acknowledged only by the end of the decade (Waldman and Walker 4). It took more than another decade until scholars of documentary film took stock of female directors.

Filmmaker and scholar Alexandra Juhasz explains that feminist-film scholars had cast documentary films and videos with realist strategies as naïve, one of the many reasons why Friedrich's oeuvre had not received sufficient attention over the years (172). Juhasz confronted feminist-film theory in the mid-1990s for overlooking documentary studies and especially its feminist and lesbian contributions. Whereas the women's movement in the 1970s had created a high number of documentaries, feminist-film scholars throughout the 1980s and 1990s argued that "realism and identification—which are claimed to be axiomatic of talking heads, cinema verité, or realist documentary—are not sophisticated, or even legitimate, formal strategies" (Juhasz 172). Their critique hinges on the claim that realism masks the production of meaning in cinema and that identification reproduces the illusion of the coherent individual (Juhasz 172).

Friedrich's use of autobiography also countered the trend of deconstructive queer strategies (Juhasz 182). Against dominant theoretical paradigms, Juhasz forcefully asserts that realism and identification in political documentary subvert the imposition of a dominant reality by representing alternatives to move spectators to "anger and action" (175–76). Friedrich's inclusion of documentary film in her oeuvre and of documentary aspects in individual films questions the notion that queer cinema's playful and deconstructive aesthetics supersede the supposedly previous essentialist and realist characteristics of gay and lesbian cinema.

Activist Formalism

Exceeding the presumed binary of documentary and experimental modes, Friedrich's *First Comes Love* integrates both aesthetics with an emphasis on editing and a decisive political stance against discrimination of gays and lesbians. Friedrich cuts from footage of four weddings outside churches in New York City to a written list scrolling on the screen that catalogues countries in which gay and lesbian marriages were illegal in 1991. Making use of "the greater depth of focus, clarity of images, and variety of field" available on film, *First Comes Love* includes footage that Friedrich shot but that appears like home movies as it lacks visible careful composition (Holmlund, "When Autobiography" 134). Similarly, the use of typescript continues her practice of relating words to images in ways that require spectators to become active interpreters of the relationship between what they see and what they read. Yet, different than her previous films, *First Comes Love* employs the written word not for poetic means but to confront audience members with facts that inflect their experience of the sound and image tracks.

This film advances in an explicit three-part composition. Part 1 depicts the arrival of wedding couples and their attendants on the steps of the church. After the first part, which lasts eight minutes, part 2 lists countries that did not allow gays and lesbians to marry, scrolling in white typescript on a black screen in alphabetical order. The third and final section depicts couples departing from church after the ceremony. The film concludes with the statement that in 1990 Denmark became the first country in the world to legalize gay marriage. A soundtrack of popular love songs enhances the emotional impact of the film.

First Comes Love displays how heterosexuality organizes normative temporality. Friedrich's cinematic strategies estrange the familiar wedding ritual and capture its role in the marking of time, which the title announces by invoking the beginning of a sequence—"first comes love." The voice-over recites the children's rhyme "First comes love, then comes marriage, then comes the baby carriage," which inscribes a chronology of presumed heterosexual maturation process. Such reference demonstrates the seemingly innocent interpellation of children into heterosexuality through simple songs with repetitive patterns.

The footage stresses weddings' representational character with anxious and happy family members and women in extravagant dresses and heavy makeup who pose for the photographer (figure 12). As the wedding couples appear with family and friends on the steps of the church in a city street, the ritual stages intimacy in public. The camera repeatedly

Figure 12. Wedding couple in *First Comes Love* (1991). Image courtesy Su Friedrich

pans across the women. The constant intercutting among familiar wedding sights, such as limousines, flowers, handshakes, back slaps, hugs, and kisses, demonstrates the time, money, energy, and enthusiasm for heterosexual wedding celebrations (Holmlund, "When Autobiography" 135). This conveys a sense of "exclusion, loss, and loneliness" for gay and lesbian spectators and a feeling of invading the familial space (Holmlund, "When Autobiography" 135). Friedrich's camerawork and its ethnographic gaze on a supremely heterosexual ritual estranges the familiar event. The popular music excessively and repeatedly invokes romance with familiar melodies, such as "Something in the Way She Moves."

Friedrich combines words and images to integrate experimental and documentary film language. The use of the written language for factual information on the screen departs from her earlier films, such as the dialogic inscription in *The Ties That Bind*. After eight minutes, *First Comes Love* cuts from the emotionally laden images of wedding parties to information on the screen explaining that different religious denominations perform "homosexual marriages" but that they are not legally binding. The austere text states: "If two men or two women wanted to legalize their commitment to each other, for any reason, they would be denied that privilege in the following countries," which ends with a colon. After this statement, which—in contrast to Friedrich's other films—is not scratched or handwritten into the film but appears as typescript, a list scrolls vertically down the screen, comprehensively identifying the nations where gay or lesbian marriage is illegal, beginning with "Afghanistan Albania Algeria Angola." The text silently appears on the screen. After the list of country names, the film returns to family and friends waiting outside the church. The newly wedded couples walk away from the altar and leave the church to the sound of the wedding march. The popular songs continue until a familiar and melancholic song—"You Were Always on My Mind"—concludes the film.

The image track yokes the songs celebrating sex to marriage. With an emphasis on 1960s and 1970s popular music, the soundtrack includes recognizable hits, such as "Get It While You Can," "Sexual Healing," and "Sex Machine." Marriage validates the pleasure of sex by tying it to familial reproduction in the context of nation-states, as they legalize and certify the union, a dynamic that was denied to gays and lesbians.[15] The exclusion of gay and lesbian spectators from the ritual exposes the sentimental staging of the wedding as a social function. The film's address to queer spectators as a community of outsiders interpellates audience members into embracing a political stance around equal civil rights.

The intercutting of footage of different yet similar couples and ceremonies foregrounds how the ritual produces gendered and heterosexual relations. The repeated shots of the brides expose the way in which they inhabit femininity as part of the marriage contract. *First Comes Love* tethers the footage of the visual excess of the scenes to the linguistic and legal decisiveness regarding state-sanctioned domestic unions. The four different weddings are difficult to distinguish from each other as the editing highlights the sameness of their rituals. Such strategies echo Butler's emphasis on performativity in *Gender Trouble*, which appeared in the year prior to *First Comes Love*. According to the queer-studies scholar, repeated gestures naturalize gender but also highlight its construction when subjects, or films for that matter, foreground its performative nature. Friedrich's film undoes that naturalization by emphasizing the repetition across different weddings. Yet, with its two meanings as the execution of an action and a public presentation, performance is not only a key concept in gender and queer theory but also in documentary (Waugh 223). Friedrich's use of the performative aligns with early lesbian and gay activist documentaries that eschewed standard realism because the desire for change led filmmakers to prefer performance strategies to express that the personal is political (Waugh 225–30).

First Comes Love integrates two versions of feminist and queer politics that otherwise appear to advance mutually exclusive political aims: the claim to equal rights and the deconstruction of heterosexual privilege. The film expresses these aims through contrasting modes of representation that define aesthetic tension: the images of weddings celebrate pleasure, nervousness, anticipation, and suspense, while the list of countries prohibiting gay marriage appears devoid of emotion. Such information creates a critical awareness among spectators about the way in which exclusion is integral to the seemingly apolitical ritual of love, dramatically changing the perspective on the wedding footage in the film's third section. This subtle shift continues Friedrich's strategy from *Scar Tissue* onward. Distinctly different, her next film employs a documentary rhetoric.

Shared Authorship

After capturing the exclusion of gays and lesbians from legal marriage in *First Comes Love*, Friedrich advances radical lesbian activism of the early 1990s with *Lesbian Avengers Eat Fire, Too*, which she codirected and coedited with documentary and television director, producer, and editor Janet Baus. In an interview with documentary filmmaker Caroline Berler, Friedrich describes the collaboration: "We decided we would coedit the film. She was more the director. [. . .] I would say she was more the choreographer of the material" (115). *Lesbian Avengers Eat Fire, Too* presents collective activism in front of the camera and relies on collaboration in its making. The group's members, including Friedrich, provide multiple perspectives on their experience of political activism for a timeline that spans nine months, from September 1992 to May 1993.

Friedrich credits her collaborator Baus for the film's idea and format, particularly its documentary style that captures the collective activist, guerilla, and deconstructive strategies of the Lesbian Avengers. In relation to Friedrich's oeuvre, the shift from analysis to advocacy and activism aligns with a move from an experimental- to a documentary-film language, including from avant-garde techniques of montage, indirect references, and subjective perspective to realism, talking heads, and cinema-verité-style shooting in the streets. Friedrich shares with other lesbian feminist filmmakers, such as Hammer, a turn to documentary (Keller 3). The film importantly presents the group's dual activist strategy of continuing traditional models of organizing, on the one hand, and exploding conventional politics with anarchic action, on the other. Departing from Friedrich's previous introspective explorations of family, memory, and lesbian desire, *Lesbian Avengers Eat Fire, Too* radicalizes the political commitment of *First Comes Love* with a call to action.

The film interweaves three threads: conversations with the participants of the New York City chapter of the Lesbian Avengers, guerrilla camera work during their political actions, and interviews with New York City pedestrians about what they imagine "Lesbian Avengers" means. *Lesbian Avengers Eat Fire, Too* cuts between footage of public actions that interrupt everyday life and group members' individual thoughtful and self-reflective responses to interview questions. The film introduces the overarching political philosophy and individual experiences of the participants while it provides a documentary chronology of their creative demonstrations and publications.

Lesbian Avengers emerged from the context of activism around AIDS in New York City, which also brought about other groups, such as ACT UP and Queer Nation. In response to the crisis, gay-rights organizations abandoned the politics of respectability and, instead, loudly voiced demands with diverse guerilla tactics. In the film's interviews, chapter members emphasize how they value the group's focus on concerns pertaining specifically to lesbians. Thus, while the deadly threat of the AIDS pandemic radicalized gays and lesbians, the latter also worried that their interests had been subordinated to the survival of gay men. The Lesbian Avengers combined creative and anarchic tactics with traditional political strategies, forming chapters, participating in demonstrations, and writing, printing, and distributing leaflets. The name Lesbian Avengers claims specific identity and simultaneously implies an ironic stance.

Participating in the movement was both life-changing and challenging to its members. Some interviewees recount how they had to muster up courage for their public activities. According to the personal memoir by former member Kelly Cogswell, the transgressive actions shattered taboos and transformed them individually and as a group (29). Cogswell describes her experience in the group: "And these early actions, with their rituals changing hate and fear into a kind of resolve, bound us together in ways I didn't understand until a long time after the group itself combusted" (26). Yet, Lesbian Avengers was not beyond the challenges of systemic inequity, access, and participation. In the film its members appear diverse regarding age, race, and ethnicity, including white, Latina, and African American lesbians. According to Cogswell, however, with increasing popularity, the number of white and younger members swelled and conflicts about race would shake the group in the years to come. The film, therefore, captures a specific historical moment.

The documentary depicts the 1990s as a political battleground in which advances that gays and lesbians made in previous years for anti-discrimination protection encountered a backlash from the political right advocating for so-called family values. Right-wing organizations sponsored legislation on the state level in Oregon and Colorado to ban antidiscrimination laws for gays and lesbians. These legal struggles invigorated and fueled queer activism and coincided with the rise of New Queer Cinema. At the same time, gay and lesbian characters became increasingly visible in mainstream culture. The figure of the lipstick lesbian forged a chic identity, as films and television shows, most famously *Ellen* and *Friends*, staged coming-out moments for national and international audiences. At the same time Cogswell's memoir serves as a reminder that in the early 1990s queers did not feel safe in public spaces, not even in so-called gayborhoods: "The Village was one of the most gay-friendly places in the city, and also the most dangerous, because the homophobes knew where to find us" (24). Personal experiences of homophobia bolstered the group members' commitment, sense of belonging, and need for the community that the Lesbian Avengers afforded beyond the culture wars.

Lesbian Avengers Eat Fire, Too integrates different documentary modes that resulted from revisions of conventions throughout the 1960s to 1990s. Its chronological organization underscores its dedication to accuracy. The many interviews reflect characteristics of participatory documentary, which involves "the ethics and politics of encounter," something it shares with several of Friedrich's other films, particularly the earlier *The Ties That Bind* and her later *Hide and Seek* (Nichols 182). The participatory mode emerged in the 1960s with "the advent of new technologies that allowed for sync sound recording on location" (Nichols 179). Those advances enabled filmmakers to circulate and shoot in public. Many of Friedrich's films also include aspects of the reflective mode, which considers documentary a cinematic or discursive construction. In other words, those films do not adhere to the notion of documentary solely as a mimetic representation of reality (Nichols 194). While the explicit presence of the camera evokes realism as a style, the placement of the camera among the activists offers an immersive experience of action (Nichols 195). *Lesbian Avengers Eat Fire, Too* also includes the performative mode, which relies on "embodied knowledge" and produces "subjective, affect-laden" meaning (Nichols 201). As the film reveals emotions, from joy to rage and anger, it offers a vibrant and engaging experience, inviting women to identify as lesbians and become politically active.

Lesbian Avengers Eat Fire, Too mobilizes cinema-verité conventions, which emerged from postwar political cinema, especially the films by French filmmaker Jean Rouch. It denotes a style of realism that relies on improvisation, often with simple equipment and lacking a voice-over. Friedrich and Baus's film shares with Rouch's famous precursor *Chronicle of a Summer* (1961) the use of the handheld camera in personal interactions in public spaces, especially the street. *Lesbian Avengers Eat Fire, Too* captures confrontational gestures of aggression in response to lesbian claims for visibility in the public sphere, which the camera records, for example, when the film opens with a protest march.

Demonstrating in support of the Rainbow Curriculum, which demanded acceptance of gay and lesbian relationships, Lesbian Avengers entered the battlefield of the culture wars. In the early 1990s, Mary A. Cummins, president of School District 24 in Queens, involved Howard L. Hurwitz, founder of the Family Defense Fund, "a conservative group founded to promote 'family life and public morality in New York City'" (Barbanel, 34). Cummins and Hurwitz denounced the proposed public-school curriculum as "gay and lesbian propaganda" (Barbanel, 34). The Lesbian Avengers perceived the conflict not only as being about politics but also as a homophobic denial of the existence of gay and lesbian childhood. Thus, the film opens with a march toward a school with the Lesbian Avengers wearing T-shirts that read, "I was a lesbian child," distributing balloons with the same message, and playing musical instruments (figure 13). The celebratory atmosphere reproduces and ironizes school parades, while the event also expresses serious concern about the ways in which homophobic parents and educators deny the possibility of a gay and lesbian childhood. The children are curious and

Figure 13. "I was a lesbian child" T-shirt worn at demonstrations in a school in Queens, 1992. Image courtesy Donna Binder

uninhibited, but the parents, often mothers, decidedly interrupt their interaction with the Lesbian Avengers.

The film includes other protests against proposed legislation to prevent equal civil rights for gays and lesbians in Oregon and Colorado. Measure 9 suggested adding to the Oregon Constitution a provision that intended to "recognize[] homosexuality, pedophilia, sadism and masochism as abnormal, wrong, unnatural, and perverse" (Sicgel 320). A similar ballot initiative, amendment 2, passed in 1992 in Colorado, prohibiting the state from enacting antidiscrimination protections for gays, lesbians, and bisexuals. *Lesbian Avengers Eat Fire, Too* documents how members of the group confronted Denver mayor Wellington E. Webb and entered the offices of Condé Nast and its *Self* magazine because they sell trips to Colorado. The Avengers demanded that the company stop offering tourist travel to the state. The mobile camera situated among the women creates a kinetic sense of participation for the audience. The fact that the film opens and closes with scenes of political action in the streets claims public space as the necessary site to negotiate rights and representation.

While the film employs documentary realism with on-location shooting, continuity editing, and interviews, the activities by the Lesbian Avengers in the diegesis subvert the status quo with parodic and hyperbolic events. The name Lesbian Avengers alone is enigmatic and ironic, which the filmmakers mobilize in their interviews with pedestrians in New York City when group members ask strangers about the meaning of the group's name. The movement's disruptive political action, creativity, and playfulness differ radically from previous social gay and lesbian movements that sought acceptance by adhering to respectability, for example, the homophile movement. The Lesbian Avengers ironically appropriate the figure of the "avenger" with its outdated and masculine connotations. Unfamiliar with the political group, respondents in New York City streets profess ignorance and use homophobic stereotypes. They reveal that they have never heard of the group, guess what the name might mean, or use the question as a prompt for a joke about lesbians. Yet, these brief interview exchanges circulate the word "lesbian" in the public sphere.

Lesbian Avengers Eat Fire, Too documents, produces, and recruits for a utopian vision of solidarity that relies on an ethics of collaboration.

As members of the activist group, Friedrich and Baus portray the relations among the group participants and interpellate audience members into a community of advocates for human rights. The two filmmakers could rely on feminist documentary traditions that empower subjects as coparticipants and create ethnographies in solidarity with the women whose lives they depict (Waldman and Walker 13–15). Beyond the collaboration between Friedrich and Baus, the absence of an expert emphasizes the film's commitment to grassroots organizing. Even though the directors filmed individual group members, they did not frame them as talking heads. Instead, the setting suggests their meeting space and a possible presence of their fellow activists. The film's informality reflects the group's embrace of alternative forms of activism.

The activity of "eating fire" conjures up the otherness of carnival performers from a less technologically advanced past. It infuses public art with politics in the tradition of happenings that were typical of avant-garde art in the late 1960s and that AIDS activism resurrected. Theatrical and creative tactics disrupt the status quo, and the interviews reveal the participants' enjoyment they derive from spontaneous actions. The members innovate political activism with irreverent acts that subvert symbolism with irony. For example, the character of the avenger with a cape and shield playfully appropriates the figure of the superhero. In another instance, the group delivers a paper-mache statue of Alice B. Toklas to accompany the statue of Gertrude Stein in New York City. The act lays bare the exclusion of lesbian relationships from the public sphere while demanding representation. At the event, they read poetry by Stein and living poets and waltz exuberantly. The joyful reenactment of a formal public event subverts traditional practices of monuments that collectivize individuals, condensing memory and ideological meaning through performance of rituals (Colangelo 22). Their hyperbolic activities criticize official forms of urban memorialization. Such an event calls forth a counterpublic, which, according to Michael Warner, is always part of the public (116). These publics, Warner shows, can appear light-hearted, like the Lesbian Avengers' actions that radiate the fun and artisanal do-it-yourself quality of the group's ethos.

The conventional documentary format of *Lesbian Avengers Eat Fire, Too* allows the group's anarchic, artistic, and improvisational features to come to the fore. With its chronology and cinema-verité interviews, the film contributes to an archive of lesbian activist history at a key turning point in the early 1990s. Friedrich's shared authorship with Baus acknowledges mutual influence and vision for the documentary mode and cinematic aesthetics. Expanded auteurism integrates the significance of individual films in the development of a director's life's work without diminishing the collaborator's contribution and legacy. The filmmakers' practice reflects the radical vision of collective activism by the Lesbian Avengers.[16]

Love and a Station Wagon

Distinct from the activist documentary and also made in 1993, Friedrich's thirty-one-minute color film *Rules of the Road* is intensively intimate and continues Friedrich's signature aesthetic strategy of combining documentary and experimental features. A film about a breakup, it mediates on the power of objects and their meaning for emotional and social relations. At the time, it was her "most 'autobiographical' work to date" (Holmlund, "When Autobiography" 135). Station wagons organize the story about the end of a lesbian relationship. The film reflects on freedom, mobility, privacy, and coupledom in the absence of heterosexual-marriage norms. Friedrich and her former partner used the car to negotiate labor, class, status, economic relations, and the end of their union.

Rules of the Road interweaves private memories with the representation of traffic in public, the pop-cultural soundtrack with intimate self-reflection, and the dynamic of a deteriorating relationship with the activity of solitaire. Depicting the hands that turn over the cards maintains the tactility prevalent in Friedrich's oeuvre (figure 14). From the innocuous account in the third person about the need for a car and its purchase by the director's brother, the film deepens to recount the homophobic reality of the lesbian couple that cannot easily celebrate family holidays together. Friedrich, according to Holmlund, blurs the boundaries between subjectivity and objectivity, autobiography and ethnography, thereby expanding the notion of documentary ("When Autobiography" 131). The film accompanies the symbol of the station wagon with the soundtrack of breakup pop songs into a narrative of lesbian intimacy that rejects the conventions of the romance genre.

Figure 14. Solitaire in *Rules of the Road* (1993), originally in color. Image courtesy Su Friedrich

The 1980s model of a station wagon becomes the motif for a failed love story and displaced attachment after loss. Friedrich's then-partner had bought the vehicle to commute to work. In the past the couple had shared the expense for the car but not the ownership, and they continued this arrangement after they separated. As Friedrich nervously anticipates a potential encounter with her former partner in her car in the city, the film mourns the lost relationship, the hope that the car symbolized, and the mobility that it enabled. An ode to the station wagon itself, the footage consists primarily of look-alike cars (figure 15). Friedrich's voice-over accompanies the footage with her personal memory of the relationship, its challenges and disintegration, and her reminiscences while watching for her former lover's car. The play of solitaire punctuates the rhythm of editing. The soundtrack includes fragments of 1970s breakup songs that end in sudden silence and a black screen, similar to *First Comes Love*. Like many of her films, *Rules of the Road* explores a public manifestation of a private relationship, locating the story in New York City streets.

Figure 15. Station wagons in *Rules of the Road* (1993), originally in color. Image courtesy Su Friedrich

Friedrich's voice-over encapsulates the autobiographical quality of the film, conveying how her lover purchased a used station wagon, a 1983 Oldsmobile Cutlass Cruiser. Repeated point-of-view shots through the windshield accompany stories about challenging family events, negotiating the city, arguments, conflicts, and finally the breakup. Friedrich meditates on reminders of her failed relationship as she negotiates the use of the car. She shares daily mundane conversations about where to park the car, who gases it up, and who smokes in it. The matter-of-fact tone is at odds with and undercuts any potentially dramatic impact of a love that has ended. The film claims representation of the everyday for lesbians connecting poetics and politics. As in her earlier films, the editing does not create a time-space continuum but, instead, a rhythm consisting of movement, direction, and color with repeated "panning, tracking, and zooming" of station wagons (Holmlund, "When Autobiography" 137).

As the station wagon conventionally symbolizes the nuclear white and suburban family of the 1970s, making it a symbol for lesbian loss appropriates the trope for a queer public. The necessity to share the cost for a used car reflects the fact that income for a lesbian couple is statistically less than that of a heterosexual or a gay couple. The prevalence of the station wagon as an icon of the 1970s in the early1990s creates a perspective on New York City that appears more outdated and poorer than the glitzy self-image that the city perpetuates in its branding. By tying the story of lesbian intimacy to a failed relationship and a used car from the early 1980s that the filmmaker does not own, Friedrich subverts the expectation of the coming-out narrative with the happy ending that constitutes the romantic couple. Instead of hope for a lesbian character in a normative relationship, *Rules of the Road* accentuates failure. In the place of romance, the film delivers reminiscences of tortured family gatherings, tense road trips, and negotiations about the maintenance of the car. Scholars validate queer failure as an alternative route to what heteronormative, capitalist society defines as success and futurity built on reproduction and economic advancement (Halberstam, *Queer Art*, loc. 117). *Rules of the Road* meditates on the conditions of lesbian love and the grief of its loss with an irreverent, humorous, and artistic appropriation of the icon of postwar American suburban mobility.

Lesbian Girls

Three years later Friedrich combines collaborative effort and intimate memories in her feature-length, black-and-white film *Hide and Seek*. Several interviews with lesbians make up a tapestry of memories about the ways in which they experienced and expressed their girlhood same-sex desires. *Hide and Seek* is among the most substantially funded and richly awarded of Friedrich's films, reflecting both her success and the fact that in the late 1990s, funding bodies validated queer cinema. *Hide and Seek* explores how public imaginary anchors itself psychosexually in individuals, expounding on the slogan "I was a lesbian child," which appeared in *Lesbian Avengers Eat Fire, Too* and inspired Friedrich.

Funding from Open Call of the Independent Television Service, the National Endowment for the Arts, and the New York State Council on the Arts also enabled the sixty-five minute running time. In a continuation of her collective filmmaking practice, Friedrich coauthored the script with her partner, Quinlan. In 1997 *Hide and Seek* received the Special Jury Prize at the New York Gay and Lesbian Film Festival, the Best Narrative Film Award at the Athens International Film and Video Festival, and the Juror's Choice at the Charlotte Film and Video Festival. The film enjoyed a higher production value and experienced greater public success than Friedrich's previous titles. It integrated the themes of personal family memories with the politics of exploring lesbian identity in Friedrich's typical style of juxtaposing diverse filmic modes, such as fiction, footage from narrative and useful films, and interviews. Many of the Lesbian Avengers also appeared in the interviews.

The film intercuts different threads, including a narrative in the form of an interspersed episodic plot about a young girl, interviews, and excerpts from educational films, such as *Sex Differences in Children's Play* (R. Parke and D. G. Friedman, 1973) and *Role Enactment in Children's Play* (Steve Campus Production, 1981), documentary films *Palmour Street* (Bill Clifford and George Stoney, 1951), and narrative feature films, such as *Simba: The King of the Beasts, A Saga of the African Veldt* (Martin and Osa Johnson, 1928) (see also Russell, *Experimental* 148–56). The childhood experiences coalesce to an awareness of a shared agency of desire without claiming an identity label and simultaneously question the veracity of visual representation, juxtaposing the girls' fantasies with excerpts from educational films that purport to provide insight and information. The personal memories contrast with a psychological and scientific discourse about gender and sexuality (figure 16).

Like *Damned If You Don't*, a loose and minimalist story line offers an episodic through line in *Hide and Seek*, which takes place in the late 1960s. Interspersed, the women appear as talking heads, and their voice-overs accompany footage from educational and ethnographic films as well as television shows celebrating the patriarchal, nuclear family. While memories reflect individual introspective subjectivity, *Hide and Seek* suggests shared past experiences as the film casts childhood for girls as a period at the cusp of confronting pressure to conform to normative gender and sexual identity. Several interviewees convey personal and intimate stories about family, friendship, gender, and desire with the split consciousness of their past immature selves, refracted by their current insight in hindsight. They admire their former selves for their ingenuity, often laughing about their miscomprehension of the world. These reflections contribute to the question of lesbian childhood as something that the women explore retroactively.

Figure 16. Watching a sex-ed film in *Hide and Seek* (1996). Image courtesy Su Friedrich

Repeatedly, the interviewees recall love, desire, adoration, and crushes on other girls or teachers. In one dramatic memory, a woman relates how she and her friend would tie each other up while naked, only for her friend's mother to appear in the room and demand that they end their friendship. Another woman shares her experience of feeling sexual arousal riding down the banister and being punished by her mother. Others tackle questions about gay-gene theory or reconstruct tomboy memories. In more than one response, the interviewee explains how she did not identify as a lesbian and, instead, feared the "bulldaggers terrorizing the school," about whom she had heard rumors. Despite conveying stories of loss and betrayal, the interview responses are light-hearted, fascinated with recollecting their own past selves, which seem to bring joy as the women revisit feelings from childhood. For example, one woman relates that in the absence of images of lesbians, she tore out a page from a comic with a naked character named Vampiri, which she hid under her mattress. When her mother discovered it, she accused her of the "sin of lust," but the interviewee recalls and reenacts her own main consideration about Vampiri at that time: "but she's so beautiful." Their lack of internalized homophobia empowered them vis-à-vis their parents and the world at large.

The interviews do not reveal a preformed and coherent lesbian identity. One of the interviewees, when asked whether she wanted to be a boy, responds that even though they were treated better, she did not want to be one. Others directly resist the expectation of the question to provide a narrative of why and how they became lesbians. One of them, for instance, addresses the camera: "I couldn't impose a narrative on those years." None of the interviewees provides a coherent account of a decided lesbian childhood. Instead, a multiplicity of narratives of erotic desires unfolds.

The fictional, interspersed plot tells a story about the main character Lou (Chelsea Holland), her friend Betsy (Ariel Mara), her older sister Anabelle (Ashley Carlisle), and her circle of friends. Lou (which rhymes with Su) does not care about boys. She and her girlfriends don't understand how sex works and imagine, for example, that they have to remain still for twelve hours. Lou and Betsy play in a tree house and go to the zoo with their friend Maureen (Alicia Manta), where tension arises when Maureen calls the two friends "queer." When they watch their teacher being dropped off by another woman, they talk about the rumor of her being a "lezzie." In contrast to Lou's rebellious but straight older sister, Lou's lack of interest in boys marks her as a tomboy. A concluding slumber party captures the continuum of girls' play and sensual erotic discoveries when they perform what they think is a séance that includes heavy breathing and fainting.

The interviews and the narrative offer alternative visions to queer theory's emphasis on the figure of effeminate boys and the tomboyish girls. The film's emphasis on girls and sexual agency subverts the privileging of boys in queer theory that Eve Kosofsky Sedgwick observed (140). The tomboy passes as a heterosexual girl moving through a phase and vacillates between two kinds of meaning, one linked to femininity and heterosexuality, and the other evoking masculinity and queerness (Halberstam, "Oh Bondage" 192). Because society negates female masculinity in young girls, tomboyism resists adulthood (Halberstam, "Oh Bondage" 194). Yet, girls can have intimate relationships with each other that pass as normative. The portrait of Lou's sister Annabelle demonstrates how society associates dangerous behavior for girls—unwanted pregnancy, predatory boys—with active female heterosexual desire.

In contrast to the excerpts from educational films, *Hide and Seek* stages childhood sexuality from the girls' perspectives. The film, thus, rewrites the figure of the homosexual presumed to be inherently sexual and, therefore, an adult (Stockton 283). Society perceives children as lacking sexual intentions and simultaneously implies that they are heterosexual (Bruhm and Hurley ix). As the film interweaves the narrative and interviews with clips from educational films, spectators realize the ways in which the latter produce and exploit anxieties among parents about their children not conforming to gender norms. For example, the calming male voice-over from an educational film explains nonnormative behavior as a "transition stage from the antagonism towards boys just before puberty to the next stage of falling in love with a boy." Such commentary imposes a temporal order of appropriate maturation.

The interviewees conjure up the childhood imagination of sexuality, while the characters act out desires in ways that differ from the perspective of adults. By integrating the fictional narrative of the past with the women's recollections in the present, the film foregrounds temporality. Remarkably, the narrative does not feature adult characters, thus granting agency to the children. Similarly, the interviewees focus less on their reflection on the past but more on revisiting their young selves, including their childhood perceptions of the world.

Hide and Seek invokes a community and, thus, supports a counterpublic as the memories present a shared point from which to speak and be understood by an audience, even though neither the girls nor the grown women claim a distinct lesbian identity. *Hide and Seek* demonstrates that acquisition of lesbianism does not occur in a linear process and that the women resist retroactively reconstructing their identification as such. At the same time, Lou expressly does not want to get married; in other words, she resists the expectation that she matures into heterosexuality.

Friedrich maintains her signature inscription into the filmic material. She insists on the particularity of women and lesbians and shifts between illusionist cinema and avant-garde techniques. The sentence "I'm never getting married" appears scratched onto the film to reflect

Lou's inner thoughts. Friedrich inscribes herself through the trace of her writing into the material of the film.

The collated remembrances create a shared lesbian cultural imagination that is at odds with family myths that photos often reproduce. As Friedrich repeatedly interrogates in her films, the family archive and individual memories often conflict, as secrets abound. Family photographs provide props for recollection in a private archive where they constitute sites of conflicting memories (Kuhn 14). The film concludes in the credit sequence with photos that show the interviewees as young girls, taking up the status of the photographic image as visible evidence in Friedrich's oeuvre from *The Ties That Bind*. *Hide and Seek* includes more photographs than interviewees. The names of the interviewees and those in the photos appear in the final credits and include, among others, filmmakers and critics. Friedrich consistently reveals how mass culture influences individual fantasies and how cultural production shapes the public sphere, as private and public are porous. The personal memories circumscribe a collective perspective on lesbian identity in the process of becoming when the young girls do not possess a vocabulary to label their feelings.

The film's queer temporality occurs in a narrative mise en abyme, when lesbians remember their childhood, while the girls who reenact their memories fantasize about their adult lives. Thus, neither group occupies its respective moment in time. The lack of belonging to one's own biographical moment defines lesbianism as the girls project their selves into different futures and, once they are older, reinterpret their past. They can only articulate their experience from a perspective later in life. In *Hide and Seek* the girls conjure up a future they cannot yet imagine, while the interviewees enjoy invoking moments of pleasure and desire of the past (figure 17). The possibility of a lesbian child only appears retroactively through a reinterpretation of biography. Halberstam defines queer time as "the potentiality of a life unscripted by the conventions of family, inheritance, and child rearing," in contrast to "the time of reproduction," which is "ruled by a biological clock for women and by strict bourgeois rules of respectability and scheduling for married couples" (*In a Queer Time* 5). *Hide and Seek* continues Friedrich's engagement with the temporality from *First Comes Love*, portraying a queer sense of time.

Figure 17. Looking at magazines in *Hide and Seek* (1996). Image courtesy Su Friedrich

The film initiates an archive of lesbian memories and fantasies that counters institutional and educational discourses on sexuality and gender. The film negotiates the status of archival footage and documentary as visible evidence. Sites of memory prove unstable, and lesbians recuperate and revalue their experiences, thus giving them new meaning from a later biographical perspective (Brunow 3). In the late twentieth century, theorists moved the discussion of the archive away from storing knowledge to the concept of an ongoing process that continuously creates and recreates knowledge (Brunow 27).

The film relies on a lesbian subversive gaze within the archive. Archivist Anne Maguire worked in the Prelinger Archives, and whenever customers requested copies of films and she saw sections that could be read as lesbian, she saved that footage (see "Interview" in this volume). It became known informally as "the lesbian reel." Maguire now labels herself a "ghostly archivist" (Delardi, n.p.). Historically, individual gays and lesbians growing up in heterosexual families did not gain access to communal memories, one of the reasons Friedrich repeatedly returns to the topic of individual and collective remembering to envision a future, from *Damned If You Don't* to *Hide and Seek*. Both films recontextualize, recombine, and rearticulate visual material to mobilize it for contemporary fantasies that reimagine dominant narratives and invest films and photographs with alternative, subversive meaning.

During the 1990s, and the rise of New Queer Cinema and queer film studies, Friedrich's cinema articulates specific lesbian identity. While her films integrate documentary features, they also continue her experimental strategies that she had established with her early short films. These stylistic characteristics include an emphasis on editing and scratching of the film in the context of poetics and music. Her works also continue to explore questions of queer temporality, collectivity, and intimacy, all in the service of asserting a counterpublic, often through processes of remembering. These processes endorse queer temporality. The themes of her films persist throughout her complete works. At the turn to the twenty-first century, Friedrich's oeuvre transcends the threshold from analog to digital media. Whereas the former invests in the backward look of memory, the latter captures the immediacy of the present moment. Friedrich maintains her stylistic characteristics and thematic threads yet turns to digital present tense with autoethnographic observations about her emotions, sick body, her mother, and her gentrifying neighborhood.

Digital Embodiments

In the twenty-first century, Friedrich persists in her approach of employing her biography as an entry way into critically engaging with social conditions and political economies. Her cinema not only confronts changing material, technical, political, and economic conditions but also contributes to public discourses, from the normalization of lesbian and gay identities to conversations about health disparities and gentrification. Friedrich maintains her focus on combining experimental aesthetics with an emphasis on editing, a subjective camera, a personal perspective, and the integration of different modes of documentary. Her films also reflect experiences of collective living in a neighborhood community.

Friedrich's oeuvre in the twenty-first century responds to a political landscape with the rise of neoliberalism, information technology, social media, and young activists rearticulating social movements. Despite these transformations, the relationship between the personal and the political remains steadfast at the core of her work. During the shift from analog to digital format, Friedrich continues to capture the themes of the female body, urban space, counter memory, and queer desire yet while also reflecting on processes of aging. Radically changing film production, reproduction, and distribution, the digital mode influences Friedrich's filmmaking, enabling her to maintain her stylistic signature and experiment with new possibilities.

In contrast to the proliferation of surface media culture, Friedrich uses digital filmmaking for a radical realism that stages what is paradoxically hidden in the current visual saturation: the sick and aging body, the frustrated self, and the displaced ethnic and working-class inhabitants of the urban metropole. In an interview she expresses her frustration with the inundation of visual culture: "Now everything is conveyed through a moving image. The carefully selected, thought-about, worked-over thing that we have known as films start to become part of this big swamp of images" (Camia 101). Her documentation of her own health concerns, negative emotions, and displacement from Brooklyn because of upscaling resists neoliberalism's demand for self-optimization, homogenization, youth, and optimism. Her films reveal the kinds of images—of the poor, the old, and the damaged—that the oversaturated society of the spectacle obscures from view.

Friedrich does not experience the digital turn as an absolute break. She continues the use of typescript, for example, across the analog-digital divide (see "Interview" in this volume). Even if she maintains her signature of expanded auteurism, the digital turn changes aesthetics, production, distribution, and, ultimately, also revenues for her as an independent director. Theaters discontinued the screening of 35 mm film, and only a few dedicated archivists and curators still project 16 mm film. The changes from DVDs to streaming also threaten an important source of income for independent filmmakers. Yet, Friedrich also makes use of the possibilities that inhere in digital media, such as the ease of typescript and the medium's immediacy. The unique combination of anticapitalist politics, feminist passion, rhythmic editing, attention to the everyday, use of archival material, and self-reflexive, autobiographical perspectives endures in her experimental documentaries. Digitality collapses time and space, since film no longer needs to be developed, shipped, spooled, or projected and, therefore, enables a different approach to temporality.

The feedback loop creates aesthetic possibilities, particularly productive for a self-reflexive filmmaker, such as Friedrich. Documentary and cinema-verité conventions and autoethnographic strategies in her work increase, while formalist editing decreases. Friedrich retains her concern with female bodies. The digital medium with the ease and speed of its circulation impacts the visual representation of physicality. The films in this period increase intimacy and extend it to the audience, reducing the distance to their objects. The precision of pixilation in digital images increases realism, particularly of bodies. In an environment in which curating the visual self for a semi-public is increasingly the norm, the pervasiveness, presence, and accessibility of image culture relativize the status of directors, especially those who make biographically inflected films. As digital visual culture dominates communication, information, social networking, consumption, and advocacy, moving images circulate on mobile devices and in augmented and virtual realities. Audiences are increasingly both consuming and also producing images as they have access to computerized programs. Cell phones deliver memories to their users, such that humans can outsource remembering to machines. The pervasiveness of ever-present visual culture produces a different context than the immersive and collective viewing experience of projected film in a darkened movie theatre.

Friedrich, like other independent filmmakers, confronts this visual culture, in which autobiography, temporality, self-reflection, and the definitions of private and public have assumed new meaning and valences. Counterpublics now exist in sedimented virtual communities on the internet and new-media platforms, which promise proliferating authorship and democratizing access for participants engaging in processes of remediation. The boundaries between the personal and the political are eroding. As contemporary culture thrives on representing and circulating private lives staged for public consumption, the representation of the personal has lost its taboo-breaking force. In this context Friedrich remains true to her values from the second women's movement and lesbian activism at a time in which neoliberalism and technology have transformed the public sphere. As an auteur her life's work constitutes an archive available for a younger generation of queer activists that demonstrates the imbrication of politics and aesthetics. These diverse yet intersecting contexts frame Friedrich's films in the twenty-first century.

The Filmmaker as Patient

The Odds of Recovery (2002) is a case in point. It focuses brutally on a series of injuries, bodily pains, and operations that have tormented Friedrich over decades (figure 18). Radically exposing her bruised body and intimate problems, she reveals her history of consecutive illnesses and unfolds a scathing critique of the medical establishment. In the form of a video diary, Friedrich describes and films her physical ailments and doctors' visits. The verité guerilla style of filming from unconventional angles in doctors' offices immerses the audiences in the immediacy of her experience, even as Friedrich recounts past operations while sharing photographs of her younger self. As is typical of Friedrich's style, written text documents different procedures over the years, from operations addressing problems with her ACL, biopsies, and high hormone levels to abscesses and infections that are results of medical interventions. The narrative accompanies a clinical account of doctors' misdiagnoses, misunderstanding, and lack of attention and care. Knowing that the scars, swellings, and infections of Friedrich's body are real affects viewers on a visceral level that can make spectatorship of the film an experience of

Figure 18. Su Friedrich in *The Odds of Recovery* (2002), originally in color. Image courtesy Su Friedrich

enduring queasiness. Such realism evokes discomfort and reflects ethical filmmaking, highlighting violent neglect, distance, and inattention from the medical establishment (see Kyröla 319). Yet, "unwatchable" films, an aesthetic category of discordant or painful images that address spectators' critical, affective, and ethical faculties, have a political potential (see N. Baer et al.). In its sustained depiction of successive illnesses, the sixty-five-minute film invites audiences to share Friedrich's experience of her body being at the mercy of doctors, who repeatedly misdiagnose or fail to diagnose her symptoms altogether.

The Odds of Recovery exposes systemic indifference to individual patients. Friedrich repeatedly recounts her medical biography only to confront formulaic repeated inquiries from medical staff and doctors. She reads her files and cites medical textbooks and self-help advice in her voice-over. Yet, in contrast to traditional documentary convention, her narration proliferates in multiple roles and perspectives instead of performing an authoritative commentary espousing truth. For example, in the opening, Friedrich addresses the camera while waiting for her physician in the examining room. Again and again, the setting situates audience members with Friedrich alone in a confined space where she undresses or lies on an examination table. This perspective aligns spectators with Friedrich, who finds herself in a situation familiar to most patients: isolated and waiting while stripped of authority, dignity, and identity. Sometimes, the camera is visible, positioned on shelves in doctors' offices and hospitals; at other times, Friedrich carries it when she walks from one location to another, filming hallways from low-angle points of view. Health-care workers ask questions from off-screen but rarely appear in the frame. The camera reveals their hands or a part of their arms or white coat, transforming them into disembodied phantoms of a medical machinery.

The film continues Friedrich's strategy of combining documentary footage with other material, including written text, contrasting sound to image, and intercutting seemingly incongruent themes, such as medical procedures and domestic activities. In this realist mode, the film shows Friedrich preparing for operations, recovering after surgery, interacting at the doctor's office, and reflecting on her nude and healing body in front of the camera. Visits and conversations with physicians organize the narrative. Friedrich's voice-over recounts her medical history and confronts the doctor's lack of knowledge and interest. She comments on questions while she is completing paperwork during intake procedures. Her descriptions of disabling pain contrasts with doctors' platitudes.

Continuing her characteristic formal editing strategies, Friedrich interweaves a chronological narrative of her operations with close-ups that expose the process of creating a piece of embroidery. Over the course of the film, brief sequences portray hands completing needlework, revealing a decorative reef of ovaries attached to a stem with leaves to create a flowery decoration. This artisanal activity that results in an organ-garland relies on everyday tactile and warm materials that contrasts to the high-tech medical machines in alienating surroundings and simultaneously ironizes domestical activity. Combining emotionally challenging footage of doctor's offices with pretty imagery, the recurrent return to the progressing embroidery creates a parallel temporal track to the film's chronological account of the director's operations. Friedrich punctuates the rhythm of the film by showing the progress of the embroidered image in regular intervals, like the way in which she presents the miniature house in *The Ties That Bind* and solitaire in *Rules of the Road*. The completion of the decorative piece occurs in the forward progression of the film's present tense differently than the chronology of her operations, which begins in the past with photographs documenting her injuries from 1977 onward.

Friedrich self-reflexively insists on filmmaking as craft by repeatedly including her hands on the screen throughout her oeuvre. Traditionally, embroidery, part of women's artisanal activity, aestheticizes the home. The manual labor of such decorative craft transforms the useful into the ornament. Film theory denounced the pretty image associated with gender, sexuality, racial, and ethnic alterity in contrast to the classic sublime or anti-aesthetic of modernism (see Galt). The visibility of artisanal work on screen in conjunction with the importance of editing for her filmmaking practice is reminiscent of the footage of editor Yelizaveta Svilova cutting film stripes in a montage sequence in Bolshevik modernist director Dziga Vertov's *Man with the Movie Camera* (1929). Vertov interspersed Svilova's work at the editing table with the footage of a woman sewing a piece of cloth and of spools of factory weaving to highlight the proximity between those two practices.

The Odds of Recovery shatters the taboo surrounding the representation of the infirmed female body. It upholds Friedrich's project of making the personal political in reconstructing a biography punctuated by surgeries. This offers an intimate life narrative that differs from a public account highlighting achievements. Following the convention of documentary, dates organize the chronology by listing her procedures: "Operation number one: November 20, 1977, age 22." The clinical accounts, the repetition of surgeries, the minimal improvement, and the slow pace subvert an expectation for healing, which often defines feature films about sick bodies. As one unresolved health situation follows another, the film neither inscribes the doctor as the healer-hero nor the patient as warrior-victim.

Counterbalancing the doctors' visits, the film includes vignettes of the lesbian couple's domestic life, especially of gardening. Depicting the prosaic normalcy of a lesbian relationship in the mundane everyday is a political act. Digital filmmaking lends itself to record the daily experience beyond the doctors' offices and hospitals. Friedrich travels through New York City on the subway, cooks in her kitchen, or works in her garden. She traverses the urban environment to visit different doctors, desperate to receive a diagnosis and successful treatment for her medical problems. The voice-over also chronicles how Friedrich moved in with her partner, who introduced her to cooking and gardening. Footage of their activities in their yard appropriates domesticity for lesbians in contrast to the second-wave feminist movement that had linked it to women's oppression since Betty Friedan's 1963 feminist classic *The Feminine Mystique*.

The film also reveals intimate details of Friedrich's challenging sexual life with her partner. Her medical problems affect her love life by diminishing her desire. However, the film rarely ventures into the interior space of their home, and her partner does not appear on camera. As a result, Friedrich extends intimacy to the audience while retaining the privacy of her partner. The contrast between the domestic personal space and doctors' visits demonstrates how the medical establishment ignores lesbians, even though Friedrich repeatedly answers questions about her relationship status. Viewers know more about Friedrich's love life and medical conditions than the health-care providers whom she encounters and from whom she receives treatment. The accounts of the challenges to her sex life contrast to the psychological literature that the voice-over recites and that ignores same-sex desire. Friedrich's focus on health concerns reflects the aging process of her generation of feminists. She continues her confrontation with midlife more explicitly in her next film in the form of a video diary, *Seeing Red* (2005).

Self-Reflection in Color

In *Seeing Red*, a twenty-seven-minute film she made after turning fifty, Friedrich speaks directly to the camera that she points at herself in what she calls "a sort of diary format" (Muhlstein 61). After expressing her frustration about her inability to change her personality traits, she voices irritation with herself and others. Friedrich conjures up benign scenes of the everyday life. In a voice-over she conveys her exacerbation: "I work myself up. . . . [I become this] maniacal person. . . . I launder the napkins." Addressing the camera, Friedrich aims to capture the immediacy of emotions in the moment of feeling them, while sharing how the presence of the camera undermines an authentic account of herself. By the time she has set up her equipment, her mood has changed, and she experiences a new set of emotions. For example, when she wants to cry because the taping does not work as she wanted, she considers that this might be good after all because her feelings might appear authentic on camera. Subsequently, Friedrich criticizes herself and complains that for most of her life she performs for other people and that she is sick of it.

Seeing Red investigates the expectations of gender and age-appropriate sentiments. The film's intimate self-portrait counters the notion of woman's nature as caring and accommodating. It centers on the color red as emblematic of passion and aggression. Friedrich's frustrated raging belongs to ugly feelings, which contrast to the demand of art to uplift spectators into the sublime (see Ngai). Instead, Friedrich articulates prosaic feelings, such as envy or paranoia (see Ngai). She recounts her minor emotions, for example, irritation instead of anger, and envy rather than jealousy. Envy results from lack of access to power. Friedrich becomes irritated with her own feminine emotions that differ from the video's theme of "rage," a taboo for women.

Friedrich meditates on the fact that her feelings are both a vehicle for and a hindrance to authentic self-representation. She employs her own voice in complex ways as she continues her signature rhythmic editing of different images with the soundtrack of Johann Sebastian Bach's "Goldberg Variations" (1741). The color red serves as a leitmotif to connect diverse objects. When she speaks directly to the camera, we see her midsection while her head is off-screen. Friedrich uses her voice in two ways. She addresses the camera in the moment of shooting and embodies her frustration with her synchronized voice on screen, and her discmbodicd voice off-screen reflects a presumably later moment. Throughout her work Friedrich remains interested in severing image from sound and recombining them in unexpected ways. In *Seeing Red*, she focuses these strategies onto her own subject position, on the one hand, and contemplates on the possibilities of the digital cinematic apparatus, on the other.

The collage of red objects moves the film into social and aesthetic frames. The color red connects the different visual objects: a dress, a bag, a neon sign, a sweater, shoes, and a bike—all of which appear innocuous and not related to anger. These everyday objects do not express the emotional valences of the film's discourse and, thus, evoke curiosity and puzzlement. Objects reappear in different contexts, continuing Friedrich's interest in repetition with variation from her early experimental films, such as *Cool Hands, Warm Heart* and *First Comes Love*. Yet, posing the question about the emotional valences of things from *Rules of the Road* onward maintains the commitment of experimental cinema to compositional principles. The film concludes with Friedrich removing the different layers of red clothing she is wearing, revealing herself swiveling in a chair in a black bra. As an artist, Friedrich does not limit herself to creating a video diary to chronicle her daily activities. Instead, she mobilizes the medium's possibility to engage in a public conversation through an immediate feedback loop, self-reflection, and by posing the question about the emotional valence of objects on-screen.

Friedrich's use of the immediacy of video differs from its mainstream use, which aims to curate the self for voyeuristic consumption with the goal of increasing numbers of viewers. The aesthetics of video diaries—conveying one's intimate affairs directly to the camera and the implied audience—have increased exponentially on reality television and, subsequently, social media. The film marks a moment in the media archeology of experimental cinema in which access to a new medium generates innovation. As Friedrich documents her engagement with aging in a changing media landscape, this short film maintains her commitment to making herself vulnerable. In *Seeing Red*, photographs of her other films appear in the mise-en-scène's background on the wall behind her, identifying her as the director of an entire oeuvre dedicated to articulating intimate matters aesthetically for a counterpublic.

Documenting Urban Displacement

Friedrich continues confronting political and cultural economies with subjective and self-reflexive filmmaking with her film *Gut Renovation* (2012). The film mobilizes "guerilla filmmaking" to expose politics of gentrification (Misra and Samer x). Friedrich shot the documentary with a mobile "Panasonic standard-def video camera" that she took into the streets, reminiscent of her early films, such as *Cool Hands, Warm Heart* and *Rules of the Road* (Segura 77). The film clearly circumscribes the perimeters of the Brooklyn neighborhood of Williamsburg and chronicles the years 2006 to 2010, during which the neighborhood underwent hypergentrification, coinciding with the 2008 financial crisis (figure 19). The upscaling forced Friedrich to leave the neighborhood, and the film captures processes of gentrification familiar to "people in big cities everywhere" (Segura 77).

As do her other films, *Gut Renovation* interlaces the personal and political, private and public. Artists, Friedrich included, had benefited from affordable living space in Brooklyn and forged a creative community. Feminist anticapitalist critique transformed the private sphere throughout the 1970s and the 1980s through collective living. Friedrich shared a former factory loft with her partner and other, often queer, artists. Such subcultural lifestyles continued even though dominant politics gutted social-welfare states and instituted conservative and neoliberal policies associated with the trifecta of Ronald Reagan, Helmut Kohl, and Margaret Thatcher, whose overlapping reigns from 1982 to 1989 defined the decade in the cultural imaginary. While several of Friedrich's earlier works invited viewers to infer politics from her experience, *Gut Renovation* foregrounds the social dynamics of gentrification with Friedrich's life in the neighborhood coming to the fore as the narrative unfolds. The film concludes by detailing the loss of Friedrich's studio loft. Friedrich, with her partner, Quinlan, and Martina Siebert transformed a floor of an abandoned factory into a "communal place where

Figure 19. Construction site in *Gut Renovation* (2012), originally in color. Image courtesy of Su Friedrich

they lived and worked for many years while the neighborhood changed around them" (Steinberg 80).

Friedrich foregrounds her emotions from the outset, which include shock about her neighbors being forced to move and disgust at affluent people flooding into the neighborhood. With rage she reacts to the dynamics of capitalism or its agents who tour the streets. Even though she captures objective facts and history, she does not inhabit a neutral position. The film alternates regular interludes of counting the destroyed buildings on a photocopied map with a marker, listing the displaced small industries and new condominiums in alphabetical order, engaging in conversations with neighbors and undercover interviews with realtors, documenting the destruction of the building across from Friedrich's own window, recounting in a voice-over her own move from the neighborhood, presenting the legal and political backgrounds, and showing newspaper headlines announcing the financial crisis.

The film connects the private loss of a community to the broader dynamics of neoliberal urban transformation. In 2005 New York City rezoned 170 blocks of the waterfront in Williamsburg and Greenpoint, which caused subsequent gentrification, a practice that the city applied under the administration of New York City mayor Michael Bloomberg, to "more than 40 percent of the city" (Moskowitz 178–79). The process allowed development companies to construct high-end condominiums. Landlords evicted small companies and renters in former factories or created rent pressure on residents. Private companies donated to the parks department to turn a park on the neighborhood's waterfront into a food-stall venue (Moskowitz 178). The city upgraded the L train to run every few minutes during rush hour, ending in a "Miami Beach-esque bonanza of consumerism," which made parts of Brooklyn more expensive than lower Manhattan at that time (Moskowitz 178).

Friedrich not only offers a personal account but also provides context for the history of the small factories in Williamsburg. The film indicts collusion of corporate companies and government that destroys the character of the neighborhood (Lugo 73). It opens with a black-and-white historical image and the original handwritten inscription "Hecla Iron Works, Brooklyn, New York, 1908." Soon, the film captures the outside of a factory building in its current condition. Typical for late nineteenth- and early twentieth-century industrial construction, the large factory consists of dark-red brick, iron pillars, and large windows. Pedestrians in light summer clothing passing on the street indicate the integration of the factory in a mixed industrial and residential urban environment. The ground-floor windows are boarded up. Recently arrived urbanites park their new, expensive cars on the street and bring with them a suburban logic that differs from neighborhood habits of communal living. New apartment buildings include gyms and spas, so that its inhabitants may limit their interaction with the outside world (see Moskowitz) (figure 20).

Friedrich's voice-over connects her experience of gentrification to its political sources. She recounts the attraction that an industrial loft had in 1989. Artists moved into the working-class neighborhood of Williamsburg, received commercial leases to which the city turned a blind eye, and renovated the spaces with their own funds. The factual policy background and description of the social-cultural shift that occurred in Williamsburg appear as text on the screen, informing audiences that on May 11, 2005, the city rezoned the neighborhood from an industrial area to residential development. The text states on subsequent screens:

Figure 20. New buildings in *Gut Renovation* (2012), originally in color. Image courtesy of Su Friedrich

"Within days, developers swarmed in," followed by, "Motivated by all the great tax breaks, they began to acquire, evict, and demolish buildings throughout the neighborhood." The next shot shows Christmas tree decorations with the year scrolling past, a sequence that the film repeats in regular intervals to indicate the passage of time. The voice-over delivers a subjective, first-person narrative that counts down to the end of their lease: "We had three years left on our lease, but I was beginning to wonder 'was I a dinosaur looking at the first snowflake?'" Friedrich highlights and tallies the destroyed buildings from 40 to 170 on a photocopied map of the neighborhood, to which she returns fifteen times during the film, visualizing the encroachment of the construction companies (figure 21).

Friedrich's personal experience charts the changing neighborhood. She documents the displacement of artists, artisans, craftsmen, shopkeepers, and small-business owners who value recycling, repair, and small-scale production. They bake bread, sell meat, and repair forklifts and buses. *Gut Renovation* gives voice to an integrated economy

Figure 21. Mapping gentrification in *Gut Renovation* (2012), originally in color. Image courtesy of Su Friedrich

advancing craft and measured consumption and serving the community. For example, Frank and Eddie's company repairs forklifts for local businesses. Friedrich documents the cleaning out of the store and the subsequent demolition of the factory building across from her window. The film lists small businesses and industries of Williamsburg by editing together shots of their signs, indicating the diversity and individuality of their styles. In the middle of that visual inventory, Friedrich shares an account about a formal report analyzing the waterfront that documented that artists and workers integrated into a well-functioning social economy.

Staged receptions for apartment viewing contrast with farewell parties of artists and highlight the process of upscaling. The butcher relates that his lease has not been renewed; the Tribeca bakery must leave; the auto-repair shop will be razed to give way to coffeeshops and bars. "It was madness"—written on the screen—expresses anger at political and economic development and her own precarity. The film embeds an ethnography of an upper-class habitus that displaces the lower-middle-class, homegrown population mix with the construction of new condominium buildings. Friedrich's camera points at designer dogs and nannies with little children in upscale strollers, training the audience to recognize the contrast between the pushed-out inhabitants and the newcomers. In other instances, Friedrich aggressively engages with recently arrived residents who do not want to be filmed or point their cell phones at her in return, such as when a group of businessmen walks down the street. The film provides insight into the creative and artistic grassroots culture at the point when investments displace them. In the latter half of the film, Friedrich highlights her own experience. The destruction of the building across the street appears in intervals, and the film turns its attention to the interior of Friedrich's loft. When inspectors visit the apartment, they accuse Friedrich and her partner of unsafe repairs and turn off their hot water. Friedrich and her housemates may remain until the end of their lease, but neighbors leave, one after the other. Photographs of past celebrations highlight the obliteration of an exuberant and creative culture, intercut with images of the slow demolition of the old factory outside, during which a big boulder in the middle of the construction site becomes an emblem of resistance. The end coincides with Friedrich's departure from the now-empty loft, final shots of parties at a new condo, and a fade to black. Before the credits Friedrich ponders about a graffiti that she had created on a wooden construction site fence: "Artists used to live here." The phrase continued to circulate on digital platforms about Williamsburg. The personal film echoes Friedrich's life cycle.

Fading Memories

Friedrich's *I Cannot Tell You How I Feel* (2016) returns to her relationship with her mother and traces the process of aging in the digital medium in a deeply personal short observational documentary. The forty-two-minute film expands on Friedrich's aesthetic strategies and themes from her earlier films. Audience members familiar with Friedrich's work recognize her mother, in part, based on her German accent. As her parent is aging, the siblings move their mother from the home where she lived independently in Chicago closer to them in New York City. In the opening the camera travels through the different rooms of Lore Friedrich's apartment. The siblings prepare her relocation, looking at apartments and studios. Friedrich goes for walks with her mother and sits at the pool in her assisted-living facility. The film's episodic structure reflects immediate moments, echoing the sensibility of memory loss.

As in Friedrich's earlier films, *I Cannot Tell You How I Feel* integrates 1970s popular songs, interviews, reflections, and typescript on the screen. Like in *The Ties That Bind*, the subjective statements in written texts on the screen do not originate from an identified speaker or a location. In instances the typescripts accompany what Friedrich expresses in the voice-over; on occasion they add and provide access to her thoughts, and at other times they speak to spectators directly. These varying forms of address create an intimate relationship with viewers, engaging them in confronting the challenges of supporting aging parents and questions of ethics of care.

Footage of Friedrich's family moving her mother in the present and material from her earlier *The Ties That Bind* reflect the passage of time. The sections from *The Ties That Bind* show Friedrich and her mother in some of the same locations as in the current film. The intertextual references tether together the films that Friedrich made at different moments in her career and highlight the biographical chronology that undergirds her work. Yet, while her earlier avant-garde analog film *The Ties That Bind* engages both the mother's and the daughter's memories and retraces the past in footage that Friedrich shot in Germany, the digital *I Cannot Tell You How I Feel* is radically set in the present with references to the past only in snippets from the earlier film.

The Making of an Oeuvre

Aging and life-cycle transitions expand the notion of intimacy in Friedrich's commitment to the notion that the personal is political, engaging core issues in twenty-first-century life, such as income inequality and health-care disparities. Each of Friedrich's films uniquely expresses a coherent artistic vision unto itself while contributing to an archive that translates the personal as political into a cohesive aesthetic. Her earliest films *Cool Hands, Warm Heart*, *Scar Tissue*, *Gently Down the Stream*, and *But No One* articulate gender and sexuality in artistic ways that queer studies theorizes a decade later. Similarly, she engages with personal and collective remembrances in *The Ties That Bind*, *Damned If You Don't*, and *Sink or Swim* before memory studies validates alternative accounts to historical master narratives. Throughout the 1990s she advances a critique of patriarchal heterosexuality in her films *First Comes Love*; *Lesbian Avengers Eat Fire, Too*; *Rules of the Road*; and *Hide and Seek*, films that claim queer temporality, articulate explicit lesbian identities, and capture the work of memory. In the twenty-first century, Friedrich continues her defining style, confronting and critiquing the effects of neoliberalism, by attending to the discarded, the sick, and the aging. *Gut Renovation*, *The Odds of Recovery*, *Seeing Red*, and *I Cannot Tell You How I Feel* address political dynamics through the lens of her personal experience.

A second-wave feminist, Friedrich belongs to a generation whose political achievements and cultural production created a legacy. The members of her cohort deserve still more scholarly attention as individual directors, cultural workers, activists, writers, and performers in their own rights. The generation actively shaped politics and culture while demonstrating that subjects are embedded in their historical moments. In her filmmaking process Friedrich redefines the meaning of the political, sometimes showing how men and women occupy public space differently, as in *Scar Tissue*, at other times shouting at investors from a rooftop, as in *Gut Renovation*. In her embrace of experimental, narrative, and documentary modes, Friedrich sustains her cinematic signature across genres and conventions, including her rhythmic editing and manipulation of film strips.

A return to Friedrich's feminist experimental cinema from the late 1970s and throughout the later decades of the twentieth century, therefore, opens a new perspective onto the relationship between film and theory, in which the former influenced the latter in previously unacknowledged ways. Similarly, her films throughout the twenty-first century address topics such as health disparities, aging, and gentrification, that are attracting academic traction as scholars recognize their urgency in such fields as disability studies. Several important books have returned to the cultural work of lesbian feminist activism from a post-queer moment, revaluing the contributions of a generation (see Bradbury-Rance; Keller; McKinney; Samer). These works take into account the important paradigm shifts of queer theory in their assessment of the value of the lesbian feminist artistic, political, and archivist labor of the 1970s and 1980s. *Su Friedrich* highlights the importance of Friedrich's experimental cinema for a rethinking of that history.

Friedrich integrates politics and formalist aesthetics to address the dynamics of gender, memory, and structural inequalities. She sustains collaborative practices of queer cinema in a form of expanded auteurism as her films unsettle normative assumptions through formal strategies. The unique editing mobilizes contrast and repetition, providing neither the dialectic synthesis of left-wing montage nor the mainstream harmonious resolution. Thus, her films challenge audiences while also offering the cinephilic immersion in an otherworldly poetic and dreamlike enigmatic experience that is cinema. Su Friedrich, in short, has shaped film history by translating feminist and lesbian politics into experimental aesthetics in ways that continue to inform contemporary visual culture.

Notes

1. A note about nomenclature in this volume: With few exceptions, I use the term "film" to refer to a completed film and prefer to use "celluloid" to refer to the material of the analog filmstrip. Friedrich herself does not use the term "celluloid," and other filmmakers and scholars might use "film" in its double meaning of the product of a completed film and the analog material. I follow the convention of using the common term "digital video," with the understanding that video exists as analog and digital, a conception that I share with Friedrich.

2. There are slight inconsistencies in the title. On the film itself, the title is *Lesbian Avengers Eat Fire, Too*. On the DVD and DVD cover, as well as in imdb.com, the title is listed as *The Lesbian Avengers Eat Fire, Too*. This book follows the title of the filmography that benefited from Friedrich's authority.

3. Quinlan had run The 'temporary Museum of Painting (& drawing) in their previous home in Brooklyn and continues it in a virtual space. See http://thetemporarymuseum.com/index.htm.

4. David Lee had studied with the experimental filmmaker Hollis Frampton at University of Buffalo. For insight into the institutional history of Hollis Frampton and the Digital Arts Lab at the University of Buffalo, see Menne.

5. The museum includes digital dimensions of photos of residents from two addresses on Orchard Street. See https://www.tenement.org/explore/103-orchard-street/.

6. A remastered copy is available for view on Vimeo, *Orchard Street* (1955, 2014).

7. Friedrich approaches the dynamics of gender and the constructions of femininity from literary and photographic perspectives in a short companion piece "Mea Culpa," published in *Heresies* in 1977. Her brief text creates a collage from sources, such as *Vogue* and *Medical Times*. The blend of quotations about women's beauty regimens accompanies photographs of a butch lesbian in different clothes on a chair in poses defying notions of proper femininity. This text and photo collage epitomizes Friedrich's method of multimedial explorations.

8. The notion of the shadow and chiaroscuro lighting has been associated with art cinema since the 1920s (see Eisner).

9. *Edited By: Women Film Editors*, http://womenfilmeditors.princeton.edu/.

10. At the time, filmmakers and theorists, including Friedrich, publicly debated how best to express radical politics in film. In fact, at the second New York Lesbian and Gay experimental film festival in 1988, nine years after *Scar Tissue*, Friedrich participated in a discussion organized by Barbara Hammer about whether radical content deserves radical form (Friedrich, "Radical" 118–23; Organizers 117). Friedrich challenged the fetishization of radicalism and distanced herself from the film festival's implied imperative that "'radical' content requires radical form'" ("Radical" 123).

11. Friedrich is taking issue with Ellen Lesser's review of the film.

12. She has adapted the term from queer film scholar Lucas Hilderbrand.

13. Stan Brakhage's practice of scratching was influenced by the work of Isidore Isou, who was part of the Lettrist avant-garde in the postwar period in France. Kaira M. Cabañas describes Isou's method: "Rather than maintaining the representational integrity of found footage shots and recombining them into montage sequences, Isou changes the shots' appearance by directly drawing on the celluloid" (37). Christophe Wall-Romana claims that Isou's films were intentionally unwatchable. He claims that Brakhage "adopted the etching and scratching techniques after seeing *Venom [and Eternity]* in 1952" (174–75).

14. The actual painting was done by Cathy Nan Quinlan.

15. Elizabeth Freeman reads the juxtaposition of the soundtrack to the "virginally white-clad bride" as interrogating "the way that the wedding seems to sanctify heterosexual intercourse by erasing the individual erotic histories of the bride and the groom," reminding viewers that weddings deny "kinship to whole cultures" (7–8). Freeman distinguishes the symbolic function of the wedding complex from the legal apparatus of marriage and reads weddings as queer, including Friedrich's film. According to her, Friedrich's *First Comes Love* "unchain[s] the wedding from marriage" (5). Curiously, in the context of her argument, Freeman invokes Friedrich as a "Jewish director," an inaccurate assertation in contrast to Friedrich's explicit engagement with Catholicism and inheritance of non-Jewish legacy of the Holocaust (24).

16. The fact that collective organizational structures are not without potential conflicts came to the fore three decades later, when an artist who designed the

logo of the Lesbian Avengers sold it, with the approval of three of the founding members, for $7,000 to the clothing retailer Gap for T-shirts and donated the money to the Lesbian Herstory Archives in New York City (see Di Liscia). Other founding members objected when the limited number of T-shirts went on sale for $34.95. The conflict not only "brought to the surface complex questions about the visual language of activism—its creation, ownership, circulation, and appropriation" but also shows the challenges that emerge from a decentralized and collective organizational structure (Di Liscia n.p.).

An Interview with Su Friedrich |

The interview took place on November 17, 2019, at Su Friedrich's home in Brooklyn, New York.

BARBARA MENNEL: Let's start at the beginning. How did you become a filmmaker?

SU FRIEDRICH: I graduated from Oberlin College with a degree in studio art and art history in 1975. I had primarily studied photography as the studio part of my major. I moved to New York City in 1976, and for two years I was doing photojournalism and studio photography, but then I attended a three-night Super 8 mm workshop with David Lee at the Millennium Film Workshop. Dave had studied at SUNY Buffalo [State University of New York Buffalo] with Hollis Frampton. I was also seeing films that were interesting to me, European art cinema—for example, films by Rainer Werner Fassbinder—at the Bleecker Street Cinema. It was exciting to me, but I didn't consider going to film school, partly because I had been in school long enough but mainly because it was incredibly expensive, and I had no money.

I became a filmmaker when I realized that it was much more interesting to make films than to do photography because one could work with movement, rhythm, and multiple images. But it was a difficult decision because I had a nice camera, and I had built a darkroom in the storefront where I was living at the time. I had invested a lot in photography, and I also really loved it. The Millennium was a miracle because it was so cheap. One could rent a camera for a dollar a day and use the editing rooms for a very small monthly membership fee. There were many filmmakers who provided instruction, so I didn't need to attend film school. After some months, Dave and I became involved with each other, and for a couple of years, we were partners. He was also eight years older than me, and he was, in many ways, my mentor as I learned how to make films.

BM: Did you see yourself as part of a generation at the time?

SF: The fact that I was going to the Millennium all the time to rent equipment and to do my editing and optical printing meant that I was getting an education in experimental film. I started going to the screenings every weekend, with programs by filmmakers who were older and had a body of work. I considered them as a generation or half generation before me. I became friends with Leslie Thornton, who isn't that much older than me, but she had also gone to SUNY Buffalo. It wasn't so much a matter of age but that I was hanging out with filmmakers who had gotten a film education. They had learned how to make films, and I learned from them.

BM: Who influenced your films and filmmaking?

SF: In 1978 I would've said Maya Deren and Margarethe von Trotta. Now I'd say that there are many more people, and films or filmmakers aren't the only influence on my work because I also read a lot. Leslie Thornton and her films were very influential. Dave's films were very instructive, and certainly Hollis Frampton, Stan Brakhage, Maya Deren, Joyce Wieland, and Alan Berliner. Over the years some people played big parts in some phase of my filmmaking, and then they moved away. Others have been consistently present through the forty-one years, for example my friend the writer Cynthia Carr.

I also watched all kinds of films, including experimental films, and those taught me a lot. And it wasn't just about how to make a film. . . . The fact that I saw so many films by Fassbinder when I was going to the Bleecker Street Cinema let me know that there was a gay filmmaker who was very out in his work, and it made me think that this is the kind of film that I should be making. But I also recognized the difference, since he was making feature films in color, and I had only $7 to make a movie.

In addition, I was a member of the collective that published the women's art magazine *Heresies: A Feminist Publication on Art and Politics*. The collective consisted mostly of older artists and a few who were my age. It was important for me as a young woman who had come to New York to become a photographer and filmmaker to have these women as role models who had persisted even though women were being rejected and ignored at the time. One day I had a conversation with one of them because I had been doing a lot of production work for the magazine. I told her that I wanted to work on my films, but I was spending too much time on *Heresies*. She said, "Go and be a filmmaker; you must do the thing you really want to do and believe you should be doing." It was amazing to get that permission. I'm very grateful to her.

BM: Did you read feminist theory or feminist film theory, or did you have a circle of feminists around you?

SF: I've never been a theory person. I mainly studied studio art when I was in college. Half my degree was in art history, but Oberlin had a very traditional art history program. I rebelled against the idea of categorization, which has been an issue my entire life. For example, in a class about Baroque art, a professor might be talking about a certain painter and telling us that this person fits the criteria of the Baroque. I disagreed; I often thought that historians or theoreticians just invented these categories to discuss the vast world of paintings or films. But even then, I had a strong sense of the individuality of each person's art, so even if I could see commonalities within a group of painters who were being called Baroque, I still didn't think they should be locked into the category.

This has been the story for me as a filmmaker my whole life. Sometimes people see me as Su Friedrich the experimental filmmaker and then as Su Friedrich the documentary filmmaker. My work never fits. If somebody else is called an experimental filmmaker, it makes sense to me because of their body of work. If somebody else is called a documentary filmmaker, it makes sense. But for me it never did.

When it comes to feminist theory, I would say that I did a lot of reading early on about women's history and the new radical feminist texts that were coming out, works by Kate Millett, Ti-Grace Atkinson, Jill Johnston, as well as older works by women like Simone de Beauvoir, and I also read as much women's literature as I could find beyond the usual "accepted" writers who we'd been introduced to in school. When I was in college, the groundbreaking work by Linda Nochlin, *Why Have There Been No Great Women Artists?* was published, and it made a huge impression on me. When I started making films, I read books that were influential at the time, for example by the feminist film scholar Judith Mayne, because I wanted to learn anything I could about women film-makers. I wondered what women might be doing differently than men in the films that I'd seen my whole life. But I didn't spend a lot of time reading the more arcane theory that was being written. That's never been much of an interest for me.

BM: Can you describe your process of making films?

SF: I've made over twenty films, and each time it's different, even though there are some things about the process that are the same, or similar, in various films. I go through a process that begins when an idea comes. In the case of *Rules of the Road*, I walked out the door and saw a car that looked like our car. That's all it took. In the case of *The Ties That Bind*, I was thinking about making a film about a woman who doesn't have a home. One day I realized that it was really about my mother and the loss of her home in Germany. I went from the abstract idea to a specific story. In the case of *The Odds of Recovery*, I had too many surgeries. *Sink or Swim* resulted from reading Alice Miller's *The Drama of the Gifted Child*, which reminded me of my father.

Seeing Red happened because I was making *From the Ground Up*. My partner, Cathy [Nan Quinlan], said that I seemed incredibly bored making this film about coffee and suggested that I make something about how I really feel. I got angry, went to my studio, turned on the camera, and started talking. I ended up making *Seeing Red*. Sometimes it's by chance; sometimes it's a deliberate plan. In the case of *The Head of a Pin*, I had stopped shooting film. We were in the country, and I had borrowed a video camera from a friend, and I walked in the kitchen, and Cathy and our friend Barbara were sitting under the table looking at something. I sat down, and it was the spider. *Damned If You Don't* happened because I was living in Berlin, and one night when I was really drunk, I was talking to a friend back home, and I said, "I want to make a film about a woman who falls in love with a nun." There are lots of reasons for making a film.

I usually test out the basic idea with somebody. For example, I say to Cathy or a friend that I'm going to make a film about some topic or person or whatever and see what they say. After the idea comes the grueling process of writing a text. That usually means scribbling, then clarifying, then rewriting many times, then showing it to one or more people and finding out what they think, and then more rewriting. All along the way, there's getting lots of rigorous feedback from people. Sometimes I shoot while I write. Sometimes I wait until I really feel like I've solidified the writing before I start shooting the visual materials to accompany the text.

All that goes on for a while. Sometimes I do archival research until I finally sit in the editing room. Editing is a very long process. I work in small units. I never put the whole film together in a preliminary, loosely cut way, which is what some other editors or filmmakers do. I can only work on small sections at a time and try to get them pretty tightly cut before I move on to another part. Editing is different now than when I edited in film on the flatbed. Because of the difficulty of editing in film, I had to plan things out ahead of time. If I was cutting something to a voice-over, I would time out all the footage because I would assign certain images to one story, so I would need to know that it took a minute and a half to tell the story. I knew how many shots I had, and I would want to put them in a certain order to line up with the story. I had to figure out whether a certain shot was long enough to cover what was being said. I measured, calculated, and planned a lot before I sat down to edit.

With the computer I don't have to set up that much ahead of time. But the many years of cutting on film were important; they taught me how to edit well. It's hard for me now with my students when I tell them that they need to look at all their footage. They want to click through and pick things out quickly. They see a frame that probably will work, and they use it. But you must learn your shots, you must know your footage well before deciding how you are going to put the shots together. The person sitting in the editing room with me is another important aspect.

I don't understand people who think they can make work on their own. I know people who tell me that they've just finished a film, and I go see it and realize it's not very good. If I ask who was looking at it and what kind of feedback they got, it becomes clear that they haven't gotten any feedback. People like my work and are impressed by the way it's written or the way it's edited, but they need to know that it's not just me; I'm not the one who should get all the credit. They should know that Cynthia Carr or Leonie Gombrich rewrote something, and Cathy, Janet Baus, or Peggy Ahwesh came in on the editing. They contributed a lot to the film, which is an important part of my process. Theorizing about the way women work or what the female gaze is does not help me think about the way I make a film, even if it might feed subliminally into my work.

BM: Scholarly literature portrays the generational and gender conflicts of the 1980s and especially the late 1980s as contentious. In 1989 you signed a letter to the International Experimental Film Congress in Toronto in which the young generation revolted against the older generation. It seems that in your memory it was not as contentious as it appears in the scholarship. The letter claimed that the event was not showing any work by women and that it was too expensive. The signatories were either female or gay male up-and-coming young filmmakers.

SF: I do remember the kerfuffle at the time and wanting to sign the letter, but I hadn't contributed to drafting it. In 1989 I had been involved in the experimental film world for a decade, and I had made *Damned If You Don't* and *The Ties That Bind*. They were films outside of the Brakhage/Frampton model. Sexism, homophobia, and racism characterized the experimental film world. We legitimately felt that the old guard was maintaining their command of the post too much. The Essential Cinema Repertory [1970–1975] by the Anthology Film Archives also fed this feeling, since the most recent films in the Essential Cinema series were made in 1972. It was as if the films that were considered essential stopped being made after that point, which excluded women and gay people. The conflict continued with the New York Film Festival's avant-garde sidebar. Originally, the New York Film Festival didn't isolate experimental film. *Sink or Swim* was shown in 1990 at the New York Film Festival in Alice Tully Hall [which seats 1,086], the home to the New York Film Festival at Lincoln Center, in a program with *Pièce Touchée* by Martin Arnold and *Scenes from the Life of Andy Warhol* by

Jonas Mekas. It was on the calendar integrated with the regular program, alongside Bernardo Bertolucci's new film, for example. At some point after that, the New York Film Festival separated avant-garde films from their regular program. It curated but also ghettoized and screened at the Walter Reade Theater, which is part of Lincoln Center but is so much smaller [it seats 268].

The lack of films by women was a problem, and I spoke publicly about that sexism. It's not over. The avant-garde is not any less sexist than MGM Studios. Some people are sexist, and some are not. It was no surprise to me that sexism was a problem when the Toronto event happened because I had already seen it at the Millennium and at the Collective for Living Cinema, the other New York venue for experimental film.

BM: It sounds to me as if you saw the problem, and you decried it without intending to become part of the boys' club.

SF: I don't think it was ever a matter of wanting to be a part of the boys' club. It was a matter of saying there's no reason that there should be a boys' club. Let's make it *a* club. A few women were accepted into the boys' club. They were always held up: Look, we have Maya Deren in here, and who doesn't love Maya Deren? I was glad she was in it, but the whole notion that there are people who decide who is in and who is out, and who then decide that only men are in, is the problem. The incredible proliferation of women's film festivals in the 1970s and 1980s was fantastic because those films were not being shown in the regular film festivals. Every film festival needs to include as many women as possible. We still need to right the wrongs.

When I made *Gently Down the Stream*, I was already a militant feminist. I was aware that my work didn't fit the model of the avant-garde. I was not able to show my work except at one or two places. When I made *Gently Down the Stream*, I expected people to think I was crazy because of the weird and gay dreams. Some people were a little startled by the subject matter—this was 1980, after all—but at the same time they seemed to be engaged by the film, they liked the way it looked, the way that the text was written with the images framed inside, so I would say that I "got away with" using such weird dreams because the film form was interesting. Then I made *The Ties That Bind*, an hourlong, experimental documentary. People saw me going in a completely different direction that had nothing to do with experimental film as we knew it at the time. People felt like I was doing this other thing. It surprised me. But it was never my mission to only make films that were recognizable as experimental films or to be part of the experimental film canon.

I just wanted to make my next film, which happened to be *Damned If You Don't*. I felt like I'd been mostly accepted by the audience of women, considering what my prior films had been about, even if some women didn't quite understand or like the more-experimental aspects of them, so I wasn't particularly worried about how they would react to *Damned If You Don't*. On the other hand, I had some trepidation about how the experimental-film audience would respond, but the thing is that you have to make what you have to make. You can't change your work by second-guessing whether people will like it or not. At the same time, you always have to be prepared to be surprised when that reaction happens.

When the Flaherty Film Festival showed *Damned If You Don't*, a woman filmmaker in the audience stood up and said that she didn't think it was time yet to show women on screen like I did in the sex scene. But who decides what the right time is when women creating their own images can make images of women as they see fit? I completely rejected that argument. And I'm sure some people would still see it that way and would still reject the film. But if you feel strongly about something, you can't worry about whether you're going to be rejected for thinking it. I couldn't sit around thinking, "Brakhage might not like my work because it's too feminist." You can't make work worrying about that.

My early work was deliberately made in opposition to a lot of the work I was seeing at the Millennium—for example structural films, even though some of them are fantastic. Other filmmakers didn't seem to bother to think about whether they were saying anything that anyone cared about or whether the film had rhythm or visuals that anyone wanted to see. I thought that was male. Why not put emotion into the film, why not add feeling, be more playful, why not be a little more honest? But I wasn't thinking, "If they didn't do XYZ, then I'm going to do XYZ." I knew what I wanted to do, and I recognized that it was different than what they were doing.

BM: The literature of the period emphasizes that in the 1980s and the 1990s you and other experimental filmmakers traveled to film festivals and college campuses to present your films. Do you think that this practice has changed? Did it influence your relationship to filmmaking? Did you experience traveling with your films as an extension of your filmmaking? Is that something that you're missing, or do you continue?

SF: Traveling to show my work continues. I was just at the Wolf Humanities Center at the University of Pennsylvania in Philadelphia last week. And these days it's a bit more luxurious and profitable than the first time I took my films on the road. Back in 1982 Leslie Thornton and I went to the West Coast, and it was a hilarious disaster. Even coordinating it was a nightmare since this was way before the days of computers, emails, the internet. . . . The screenings were okay, but we came home almost penniless. We had no idea how to get it done, what to charge so that we could at least break even. But it was a good learning experience. At the Collective for Living Cinema and the Millennium, most of the time the filmmaker was in attendance, and I had become accustomed to the notion that you'd see films and then talk with the filmmakers. It could be boring or interesting, and of course at times I was excited to meet a filmmaker whom I really admired.

For filmmakers getting your work out and being present at a screening or event has been one of the only ways to make money aside from having a distributor. There was more grant money when one made films than there is now, but it was never enough. And with 16 mm films, they were rented by schools or art centers. The rental fees were decent compared to what they are now with DVDs and digital, except, of course, universities still pay more for institutional-usage rights. Back in the day, when you made a new film, you'd contact a lot of people by fax or phone. You'd have to print photographs and put them in the mail. It was labor intensive, but I was very organized because of the kind of work I had done to earn a living.

I've been doing this for forty years. I traveled everywhere. Sometimes I enjoyed it, and sometimes I found it exhausting. The tradition is weird because it assumes that when filmmakers like me—in other words, filmmakers who don't make feature films for general release—show their work, it needs to be explained or discussed. Whereas if somebody goes to see a movie in the movie theater, they just leave afterwards and have a drink with their friends and talk about it. I don't know when it started. Maybe when somebody was showing a film in their loft, maybe a film by a fellow filmmaker or by themselves, and then people talked afterwards, and they enjoyed the conversation. Like most of us, I'm not always paid that well for doing all that traveling and public speaking. But sometimes the payment is generous, and it does help me to survive as a filmmaker.

BM: Do you see yourself as an auteur? Do you think you have a signature across your films?

SF: These questions are for other people to answer. The maker cannot really see themselves as others do. We don't work that way. We work from our gut or head. Something gets done and then you go on to the next thing. I don't see myself as making a certain kind of film or having a signature style. But if I look at some of my older films that I haven't seen for a while, I'm surprised how consistent certain aspects of my work are, for example, the editing, the way I write or the way I combine an image with a text. Auteurism is a strange concept because a writer has written everything that's in their book, whereas most films involve many people in the making of them, even the French New Wave films, which were what started the notion of the "auteur film." If you are a filmmaker who does all aspects of the technical work yourself, then you are the author of all that work. It's always made by Su Friedrich.

BM: I noticed especially in your earlier avant-garde and experimental films, which have a high-culture status, that they include popular culture, from bodybuilding to 1970s rock-and-roll. Can you describe your relationship to popular culture?

SF: I'm a product of both high and pop culture. When I was growing up, I was exposed to the "highest forms" of literature, theater, and music. My mother only listened to classical music. My father gave me a volume of Baudelaire's poems in French when I was in college. I was exposed to museums and serious art. But I was also growing up listening to pop music and going to popular movies, such as *Goldfinger*. You work from everything that you've experienced and heard. I don't see a problem in making something that is seen as high culture and putting in a song by Tina Turner. Those things live together. The greatest music that's considered part of pop culture, R & B, is not played at Lincoln Center. To me that is very high art. The labeling of pop culture and high culture is false because you can have the most brilliant singers—for example, Aretha Franklin—put in that category of pop culture, but she's no different in her talent than the great soprano Jessye Norman. They just come in different packages. The same is the case with films. There are high- and low-art films, but they are all part of a big mix.

BM: Your films are personal. You expose yourself, making yourself vulnerable throughout your films but especially in *The Odds of Recovery*. At the same time, you afford relatives and friends privacy. Do you think it's necessary to make yourself vulnerable to make important films? Is it difficult for you, or does it come easy? How do you think about putting your naked and sick body on display or talking about your lack of sexual desire on camera?

SF: For my entire life as a filmmaker, I've had the bizarre experience of showing a film and then having people come up to me afterward to thank me and then tell me about their father, their mother, their illnesses, and their sexual habits. Because my films are personal, people connect to them, and they come and tell me everything about themselves. When I was starting out, I considered this to be nuts, since I'm not a therapist. Then I realized that the film created a space for people to look at their own experiences. I became very grateful that I had inadvertently done that for people. I'm very respectful when somebody talks with me. If they want advice, I try to be helpful. I realized that people knew so much about me and that I didn't know anything about them. A stranger would come up to me, and they were a complete blank to me. There was this bizarre difference between how they were looking at me and talking with me, and how I was relating to them.

When I was young and doing photography, I did a series of nudes with friends and made a photo essay about women's appearances. I wrote personal material, but I was also reading texts by women about their experiences because they had not been portrayed or written about very often. I felt that we needed to get this material out there. When I made *Gently Down the Stream,* I wondered whether I might be crossing a line because I was exposing so many strange dreams. A straight Scottish man came up to me after the first screening and said that the film was fantastic and that he had dreams exactly like the ones I described. I was so shocked. I wondered how that was possible, and I walked away from the conversation thinking that one can never know who shares one's experience or who might be interested to know about it. I also learned that people translate my experience into their own. When I made *Rules of the Road,* somebody came up to me and said if they had made that film, it would've been all about red shoes instead of cars. Over the years I've grappled with the question of how much to expose myself and how much to expose other people, but I keep finding that people like that I expose those things because they've had the same experiences or thoughts or feelings.

The most important question is whether I'm being self-indulgent. I challenge myself with that question. If you work long enough and have people around you who are telling you to stop being indulgent, you learn that the initial impulse might be considered self-indulgent. But if you're working on a film, you have to go out and shoot good images, write good text, and figure out how to put it all together. This is all really hard work, and especially when it comes time for the editing, you stop being caught up in your emotions, and you just become concerned about whether one shot follows sensibly from the last one.

There is another aspect to this, for example with *The Odds of Recovery*. I started it under duress because Cathy didn't want me to make the film, and she didn't want to have anything to do with it. I had to decide whether to make it against her wishes and without her approval. I forged ahead and expected it to be a horrible experience because she always played such an integral role in my filmmaking, as a good listener, a tough critic, a great cowriter, a contributor of so many ideas, et cetera. Halfway through the editing process, she agreed to look at it, but when she saw her name on some of the title cards, she was outraged. So, I had to change the wording and call her "my companion." That was the most serious case of someone being in a film of mine and really not wanting to be in it. When it was finished, I had a one-week run at the Two Boots Pioneer Theater in the East Village. I begged Cathy to come along with me on opening night, but she wouldn't, even though all our friends were going to be there. She said that she spent so much time seeing me in hospital gowns in real life that she didn't want to see me in one on the big screen. I somehow finally understood the reason for her deep objection to me making the film and said that it made perfect sense and that I was sorry. And then, miraculously, she agreed to go to the opening, which made me so happy.

I showed *The Ties That Bind* to my mother before I finished it, but I didn't show *Sink or Swim* to my father before I completed it. I always have to take into account the people who are in the film. How am I representing them, will I interact with them while I'm making it, and how will they feel about what I've done when it's all over? It's an issue each time I make a film, and it's particular to each film, the degree to which I involve someone.

BM: Can you talk about the different modes of filmmaking in your films, from the experimental collage to narrative or documentary mode? What's your relationship to them? How do you decide when to integrate different modes?

SF: From the beginning, I saw lots of different kinds of films that were interesting to me for all kinds of reasons. Each film has a different voice. I wasn't trained to work in a certain way. Experimental films are amazing when one considers what one can do with images and sound when you aren't restricted by the rules of traditional narrative, but I also thought that narrative film was wonderful. If you aren't limited by one mode, you can use whatever you want. My first film was abstract, consisting only of images and sounds. *Cool Hands, Warm Heart* was a narrative. *Scar Tissue* was abstract, followed by *Gently Down the Stream*, in which I used text in a more experimental way than I had in *Cool Hands, Warm Heart*. And then *The Ties That Bind* is a documentary. I've always used whatever form or genre or style I needed in order to say what I wanted to say.

The Ties That Bind was going to be a documentary, but I didn't want to record the interviews as talking-heads interviews. I felt that would lock me into a much more traditional form. I was more interested in the challenge of having to find ways to use all sorts of other images over the voice instead of falling back on having the viewer see my mother speaking on camera. For *Damned If You Don't*, I didn't think about using the footage from *Black Narcissus* at the beginning, but I did plan it to be made up of narrative scenes that I shot. Of course, finding *Black Narcissus* and being able to play out that narrative against my own was very exciting. When I started to think about making *Sink or Swim*, I somehow assumed that it should be a narrative, so I tried to work up some scenes, but then I realized that was completely crazy, and it became the film it became.

Every film has had its own requirements. I was in a certain mood, or I tried something that didn't work, and then I tried something else. I have befuddled people endlessly. I began *Hide and Seek* as a documentary.

I did two-hour interviews with twenty different women because I had no money to develop it as a narrative. I transcribed all the interviews and kept telling myself it could be done entirely using them and the archival material I'd collected, but then I got the funding from the NEA [National Endowment for the Arts] and ITVS [Independent Television Service], and at first I felt like I could go back to my original dream of making it as a narrative. But then I considered how good some of the interviews were, and it seemed more interesting to interweave them with the script we were writing and the archival material I had, so I mixed them all together. When it got into the Sundance Film Festival, they didn't know whether to put it in the narrative or documentary competition. People have a problem naming what I do. But that's their problem, not mine.

Underneath these distinctions, we're always telling stories. Brakhage, who is considered abstract in his experimental filmmaking, also tells stories in his films. I was sitting in the Millennium one day watching a film of his, and I suddenly thought, "Now it's going to end." And it did. It was amazing because I thought he isn't telescoping the end. This could go on forever, and there isn't an obvious narrative with dialogue and characters being played out, but there's something in the structure and the flow of images that comes to a recognizable end point because the film is built to have a beginning, a middle, and an end.

BM: How do you think about the difference between celluloid and digital for filmmaking and distribution?

SF: By now I don't give a lot of credence to them being vastly different or one being better than the other. There are things about the way films were made when it was on film that are not happening now, of course, but I've learned that you can't stop the world from turning. When I had to stop shooting film, I thought it would be a disaster. At first it was heartbreaking to me to imagine that how I had worked in film was no longer going to be my experience, and I felt that there would be something inherent in the process of shooting and editing in digital that would no longer allow me to work in the way I had when I shot and edited in film.

However, there are things that I can do when I'm shooting and editing in digital video that I couldn't do in film. I try to use that to my advantage. For example, I used text on screen in various 16 mm films, but it's very laborious to produce text onscreen. You had to typeset the text and have it put onto acetate film and then shot on a light table, and all of that had to be done by other people, and you had to pay them. So, it was laborious and expensive, and if you wanted to make any changes, you had to go through all of that all over again. On the computer I can play endlessly with the text. This is an important part of my recent work, how I create an interplay between the voice-over and the onscreen text.

Switching from film to digital also shifted my work from black and white to color. I had made two films in color, *Rules of the Road* and *The Odds of Recovery*, so it wasn't as if working in color was completely foreign to me, but I did love black and white so much, and when I started shooting video, I imagined that sometimes I would convert it to black and white afterward, but I never have. It also made a huge change in my sound, because I hadn't worked with live sound except in the case of *Hide and Seek*, where it was obviously necessary. I didn't own a sync-rig 16 mm camera, and I wasn't even that interested in working with sync sound, but when you shoot video, you always capture the sound as well, and having that material made me get involved in working with it. Or deleting it. So, working with text onscreen more easily and shooting and editing in color with sync sound have been the consequential changes in my switch from film to video.

BM: I would like you to address *Edited By*, your website about women editors. How did you conceive of the idea? Why did you decide on editors and not a different profession? What is the relationship between your own work as a filmmaker and this kind of public educational work?

SF: I was reading a chapter on editing in a film-production handbook for my students, and it didn't mention the editors, it only mentioned the directors. I wondered why the chapter on editing was not highlighting the editors, who were the ones who did the work. When I looked them up, I discovered that many were women, which amazed me. I was ashamed that in all the years of making and editing my own films, I didn't know about these women. I knew about the few most famous American ones, Thelma Schoonmaker, Dorothea Carothers "Dede" Allen, and Verna Fields, as well as the famous male editor Walter Murch.

At that moment the world just blew open. I felt passionately that we all need to know about these many other women editors. After a year of researching, I launched the site in January 2018, and at that point, it featured 139 women. Now there are 202. I started by focusing on professional editors, women who had done all the films directed by Roberto Rossellini, Werner Herzog, Jean-Luc Godard, and so many more films in the canon of cinema. My mind was blown every day as I uncovered more and more famous films edited by women. I also felt a deep kinship with them, as if I had found "my people," but a day came when I recognized that they were, in a certain sense, different than me. They were editing films like *Star Wars* or *The Wizard of Oz*, and I edit the kinds of films that I make. So even though the same basic skills and sensibility goes into being an editor regardless of the topic, genre, or budget, I felt like I needed to create two separate-but-equal groups on the website. One section covers all the professional editors, and the other covers filmmakers who also edit. In some cases, like myself, I always edit my own films.

One of the slightly funny downsides to doing a website like this is that people keep writing me about someone I've left out. I keep learning, and that's why I spent another five months adding about 26 new professional editors to the site after the launch. I've done a few public presentations about the website because, even though people can go online, it might be daunting because there are so many amazing women in it. This is a way of talking more generally about the history and giving some examples of what's on the site.

When I finished the site, I had a launch party at Union Docs and put together a companion film. I selected a one-minute clip from a film that each of the editors worked on, and I strung them together in chronological order. The website is chronological, following the year of the birth of the editors, whereas the compilation film is organized according to the year the film was made. The first version of the film is 75 minutes long, but after I added all the new editors, I also made a new compilation film, which runs 113 minutes. It starts with *The Iron Horse* (1924), edited by Hettie Gray Baker and directed by John Ford, and ends with *The Battle of the Sexes* (2017), edited by Pamela Martin, ACE, and directed by Jonathan Dayton and Valerie Faris.

BM: Let's begin discussing individual films with *The Ties That Bind*. Was your journey to Germany a result of your intention to make this film? What is the relationship between your life and a film?

SF: When I realized that *The Ties That Bind* was going to be about my mother, I wanted to go to Chicago and talk with her. I also felt that it was imperative to go to Germany because I had never been to her hometown, so I went to Ulm, where she lived until she moved to America. I saw her house, her parents' grave, and I went to the city archive to see whatever footage they had from during the war, particularly footage of the damage after the major bombing raids. It seemed necessary that I visit her home territory.

BM: The film also suggests a connection to the contemporary moment. Could you reflect on your own activism at the time in relation to the Nazi past?

SF: The film shows a protest by the Women's Encampment for Peace and Justice in upstate New York. I was briefly a member of that collective. I also was active in politics in other ways, whether it was demonstrating about various issues or working on a feminist magazine or making posters. I had grown up with a mother who had been through the war and was now living in the United States. I understood how impossible it would have been for her to do more than she did during the Nazi period, even though in her life in America, she was a fierce Democrat and a very outspoken person. I realized that she could not act on the strength of her convictions against the Nazis when she was living in Germany because she risked being killed, in contrast to my political activism, which never posed that same threat. If I went to a demonstration in Chicago during the convention, I was not going to get gunned down or dragged off. It was sobering and enlightening because when you're young, you think anything is possible and that everybody should be a hero, including your parents. When you grow up, you realize that you're thinking that because you live in a culture where you're not going to get killed for your political activism.

BM: You already mentioned that *Damned If You Don't* originated in a moment of drunkenness. I'm intrigued by your use of Judith C. Brown's book *Immodest Acts: The Life of a Lesbian Nun* [1986]. How did you find the book? It emphasizes medieval religion more so than lesbianism. The integration of the garden in the film evokes her description of medieval culture in Northern Italy.

SF: When I have an idea for a film, I start doing research. Films about nuns were popular in the 1960s, for example, starring Hayley Mills. We used to call them "nun films" when we were kids. I looked at all of those films. During the 1980s some nuns were starting to come out and were writing about their experiences, and those were interesting to read, but I especially liked Brown's book because it was so extreme.

BM: Regarding *Sink or Swim*, the film about your father, I wondered whether there's a connection between your father's interest in anthropology and your interest in an ethnographic observation, his interest in poetry and your interest in editing. I wondered whether you are doing something similar but in a different way. Do you think of these films as autobiography or autoethnography? Or would you say that you use the example of yourself to capture larger societal structures?

SF: I don't use the word or term "autoethnography" because it doesn't apply to my films. I thought my father was despicable. He treated me, my siblings, and my mother badly. It was time to tell the story from my side. Alice Miller's book *The Drama of the Gifted Child: The Search for the True Self* argues that children's experiences are not the official story of a family. Instead, the parents provide the official version. He had caused many problems and a lot of pain, and reading her book emboldened me to describe the experiences I had had with him. Because he was a linguist, I structured the film according to the alphabet, with the title cards of the twenty-six chapters starting with a word that begins with the letter Z and ending with one that starts with A. So, in a sense, it's a nod to the building blocks of his work as an academic and particularly as a linguist. His father was a very hard worker, and both he and my father were very productive, so I would say that I inherited some of my work ethic from them but also from my mother, who was also very energetic and seemingly tireless. But I didn't read his books, so I didn't model myself after his methodology as a linguistic anthropologist.

BM: Could you talk about the combination of formal aesthetics and lesbian politics in *First Comes Love*? How does the film capture the specificity of its historical moment, and does it relate to the contemporary moment? How does it advance politics through a formal structure?

SF: I don't remember what triggered the decision to make *First Comes Love*. When people started talking about gay marriage, I considered making a film about it. After rejecting the idea of doing a lot of interviews and crafting it as a documentary, I went instead to a number of conventional, straight weddings. I wanted to work with music because I had gotten so excited about cutting to music when I did it in *Sink or Swim*, but music was also central to what I was depicting in *First Comes Love*. For every superromantic love song that you dance to at a wedding or that you've listened to before and that made you decide to get married, there's a brutal song about a breakup that you have to listen to, drunk at the bar, when the marriage is over.

As far as the structure is concerned, the film starts when the couple arrives at the church and ends when they drive away in their fancy rented limo. Throughout the film I alternated between the true love songs and the heartbreak songs. The three-minute scrolling text midway through the film lists all the countries of the world that hadn't legalized gay marriage, which was basically the whole world with the exception of Denmark. People asked me why I'd done it that way, why I hadn't filmed gay weddings or done interviews about how people felt about them. Maybe I made the wrong film. Maybe it would have been better to show gay weddings, but my point was that marrying outside the legal channels—this was twenty years before New York legalized gay marriage, so weddings back then weren't legally binding and although it was fine to be married, gay couples didn't have the same legal rights and benefits as straight couples. I wanted to show how marriage functions for straight people, how it's celebrated in such a public way, and how that wasn't available to gay men and lesbians.

BM: Do you feel the young generation of queers connects to these issues, or do you think it was an issue at the time and doesn't really connect to the current moment?

SF: I just had a retrospective in Frankfurt, and I didn't think to ask how young people felt about it, but I also didn't get any sort of negative response to it. It has shown in other venues in recent years, and one funny side aspect to the film is it's shocking to audiences that so many countries in the world have changed. There's no more Soviet Union, for example. No more Yugoslavia.

Since people now take for granted that it's legal in so many places, young viewers can recognize that this wasn't always the case. Oddly enough, the day that it became legal in New York, I was at a screening of a film by a lesbian filmmaker. She rushed up to the mike when the film ended and announced that they had just passed the law in New

York. There was a huge crowd, and everyone went wild. When we were walking home, I realized that it was exactly twenty years since I had made the film and that the fight to have the law changed had taken twenty years. Sometimes films become historical documents.

BM: Why did you decide to make *Rules of the Road*, a film about a breakup?

SF: I was living in a different apartment in the neighborhood where my partner and I had lived together, and I walked out the door one day and saw a station wagon like the one we had shared. I thought she was in it, and I freaked out. I went home and started scribbling on a little notepad, various scenes, various memories of what had gone on between us. Later I thought that I should do something with those sketches. I can't remember how long it had been since we had broken up, but I was still very upset and unhappy. I don't think that I'd been wondering about whether or not I should make a film about it. I was just so depressed, and this seemed like a specific way to talk about it. I had such a strong reaction to seeing the car, and I just went from there.

BM: You are committed to the artisanal making of things with your hands, which enhances the personal and tactile sense of your films. We often see your hands making things, like the embroidering in *The Odds of Recovery* or the building of the toy house in *The Ties That Bind*. In *The Odds of Recovery*, you talk about cooking and gardening. These motifs seem not only to reflect your interest in craft but also to comment on artisanal filmmaking.

SF: I learned to embroider and crochet from my mother when I was a child. I started sewing my own clothes when I was in grade school. I built a dollhouse with my sister because my grandfather had a wood-working shop at the farm they stayed in during the summer. During my adult life I've made many quilts, and I've also done massive amounts of construction work and renovation in the various apartments, lofts, and now the house we live in. I've always loved working with my hands. A filmmaker handles the reels of film when they load the camera, when they edit, when they run the optical printer. I liked that filmmaking was a manual job, and it seems strange to me now working in the digital world, where everything is virtual. So it seemed natural to me to show those kinds of activities in various films. It happened without me intending to make some sort of point about my handiwork.

BM: I showed *Lesbian Avengers Eat Fire, Too* to my students this semester in a class on feminist, queer, and trans theory and cinema. They appreciated learning about queer history. It's the most explicitly political and the most decidedly documentary film. Do you think that is related?

SF: The film is a fantastic record of what the Avengers did, and I'm really happy that it exists because I loved being in the group and doing all the actions. But I don't consider it "a film of mine" because Janet Baus, who was a member of the Avengers, had the idea, and other people had already filmed a lot of the actions that the Avengers had been doing. Janet set up all the interviews, and it was only later that I got more involved in the project. I suppose that the form of it is related to the content, but it's not as if Janet and I talked about the option of making it more experimental. Her background was in doing short documentaries for cable news shows like *In the Life* and *Dyke TV*, and it just seemed obvious that we would structure it as more of a conventional documentary. We did the editing together, and Janet was really good at writing the texts for the title cards. It was a lot of fun to collaborate with her.

BM: There is no history of the Lesbian Avengers, only memoirs and those films.

SF: Well, Kelly Cogswell was one of the members, and she wrote a great book about it a few years ago, *Eating Fire: My Life as a Lesbian Avenger*. She also built a website for the Avengers, which has tons of information in it. Women now might go to a dyke march in Cleveland and not have any idea that the dyke marches were started by the Avengers. For those of us who do know the history, it's obvious that it was a really important group for what it launched. It's strange to think that the film is from twenty-six years ago, which is more than a generation. And with the passing of years, it might look strange to some people, since it was about the specific experiences of lesbians, it was about making lesbians visible in a world that paid us no mind. The ensuing generation started preferring to name themselves as queer, and these days there's the greater visibility of the transgender community. Sometimes, someone will ask why the Avengers had to be only about lesbians, but back then we needed to become visible, and the Avengers were incredibly successful in achieving that. Personally, I think it's still an issue, it's still a problem, there's still good reason to address the specific experiences and concerns of lesbians.

BM: How did you come up with the topic for *Hide and Seek*? Can you reflect on combining interviews with the narrative?

SF: Because I joined the Lesbian Avengers after it had already formed, I didn't really know much about them when I showed up at the first action. It was in a fairly conservative district in Queens, and they were handing out balloons to children as they arrived for their first day of school. The purple balloons were printed with the words, "Teach about Lesbian Lives." The kids were delighted to get free balloons, and their parents were totally freaking out.

A lot of Avengers were wearing T-shirts that said, "I was a lesbian child," with an image of a girl on it. I was stunned because I was thirty-five, and I had been out for fifteen years already, and I had never thought back that far. Movies and books about coming out were important, but nobody had talked about pre–coming out. For the interviews I had access to speak to women in the Avengers and also to other women who weren't. Some of those were my friends, and some were women who signed up to be interviewed when I did gigs and told the audience about the project. Originally, I wanted to have it be a fictional film, but I didn't have any money for it. It was a couple of years after the culture wars, and the right wing was aggressive about the content of performances and films that were funded by the NEA. [In June 1990 John Frohnmayer vetoed the NEA grants for Karen Finley, Tim Miller, John Fleck, and Holly Hughes on the basis of subject matter after they had successfully passed through a peer-review process. The artists won their case in court in 1993 and were awarded amounts equal to the grant money in question, though the case would make its way to the United States Supreme Court in *NEA vs. Finley*. Under pressure from Congress, the NEA stopped funding individual artists, but Friedrich was able to apply before that restriction was put into place.]

Despite the atmosphere at the time, I applied to the NEA and got the funding. I couldn't believe it. I was emboldened. I thought, if I got past that hurdle, what could be next? So, I applied to ITVS, and by what I considered to be a miracle, I got funding from them also. Months later, when I'd finally managed to find someone who would work as the producer, I learned an interesting fact. The producers were Eva

Kolodner and Katie Roumel. They worked at Killer Films, which was run by Christine Vachon. She had to "release them" from their usual duties so they could work independently for me as the producer. I was so grateful that she would do that, and one day she told me about how I got the ITVS funding. She was part of the final panel that year, and she asked to look at who had been rejected during the prescreening process, in case there was somebody she wanted to keep in. She saw my proposal and rescued it from the pile. So, I got the money, maybe around $250,000. It was a lot of money compared to anything I have ever had to make a film. I thought, now I can also create the narrative part, and for a while I considered just making the film as a narrative, but a lot of the interviews were so good that I tried to work the two elements together. Cathy and I spent a lot of time writing the script for the narrative.

I selected the interviews and searched for archival material. My friend Anne Maguire worked at the Prelinger Archives and oversaw film orders. Whenever she would see an image that seemed lesbian to her, she would put it on a "dyke reel," which she shared with me. It was so amazing because, aside from a lot of other great stuff, it had the footage of the girls in the lemon orchard. The film it came from was about how sailors should eat lemons so that they wouldn't get scurvy . . . but what she noticed was two little girls kissing each other. I got such good footage from her dyke reel. Another example is the footage of the black girls in the playground, which comes from a documentary by George Stoney. That was a lucky break. As you can imagine, it wasn't easy to find archival footage of black children back in those days. I also looked elsewhere for other footage. I had amazing material. Between the narrative footage, the archival, and all the interviews, I had twenty thousand feet of film, and it took me a year to edit it all together.

BM: I see a thread running through your work about remembering the past and creating a fantasy of the future. *Hide and Seek* reconstructs collective fantasies, and the women remember their youth. Are you interested in individual memories, or do you try to get beyond the individual?

SF: Yes, my films are about memory, among other things. One of the unexpected consequences of working the way I do is that even if I make a film about my own memory or somebody else's memory, as time goes by those films sometimes become a reproach to me. The best example of that is *Seeing Red*. I made it when I was fifty, and in the film, I talk about how I shouldn't be doing this and that. I was recently sitting in a theater watching the film, which was fourteen years after I'd made the film, and I realized I'm exactly the same as I was fourteen years ago. A film becomes a document of something that you thought you were going to move beyond or change, and then you discover that you haven't.

BM: *The Odds of Recovery* is difficult to watch. Could you talk about the practical aspects of making the film? Did you take your camera with you to the doctors? Did you tell them that you were making a film?

SF: In the making the film, I was uncertain about how people would respond to it. In general people don't really enjoy talking about medical problems, and I was going past the limit of what is tolerable for viewers to experience by including those images of my breast all bruised. I knew I had to do that, but I knew that it was going to be unpleasant for people. I always feel sorry that audiences have to look at those hideous images, and I also always feel embarrassed about them seeing me like that.

I had a doctor's appointment about a week after I decided to start working on the film. I had a small video camera which I took with me. And you know the drill. The nurse asked me to put on a gown, open to the back, and said that the doctor would be in soon. That gave me some time, because they never come soon, so I put the camera in a sort of inconspicuous place on a shelf, turned it on, and let it run. When the doctor came in, I worried that he'd notice it, but he didn't until the examination was over. I then went so far as to ask him to sign a release form, and he did! This happened a bunch of times, and they never noticed the camera, and they all agreed to sign release forms. It was weird. I did it every time.

As for the practical aspects, I started out thinking that I would do all the shooting myself, as I always do, but it became very difficult when I was on camera. I did some of that by putting the camera on a tripod, but I also hired the filmmaker Joel Schlemowitz to do some of it, and I think he did a great job.

I did have a crazy problem during the edit. Everything was shot with my Bolex, so it was all silent, and I was fine with that. But when I was editing, it didn't work at all, so I had to go back and create sound effects for everything you see . . . gardening, cooking, et cetera, and then work them into the track. It gave me a lot of respect for Foley artists, but it was also very educational since I discovered that celery, for example, is really useful for making all sorts of sound effects.

BM: How do you feel about going back to your mother for *I Cannot Tell You How I Feel*? *The Ties That Bind* was such an early film, and *I Cannot Tell You How I Feel* is such a late film.

SF: I didn't plan to make *I Cannot Tell You How I Feel*. We had to find a place in New York where we could move our mother, and I took my camera with me to record how the apartments looked, since they tend to look so alike, and it was an upsetting experience, and things would just become a blur for us. When I was with her in Chicago for the last time before we moved her, I realized that there were things I wouldn't see again, and I filmed those moments, like her at the beach. But it took a while before enough footage piled up, and enough experiences, before I recognized that I needed to make the film about it.

It was strange that I had already made a film about her, and I wondered if it made sense to make a second one, but this was such a different enterprise that I decided to proceed. *The Ties That Bind* was about her youth, about the Nazis, about losing her homeland, whereas *I Cannot Tell You How I Feel* asks such different questions and covers such different territory. And it was interesting because making the new film and being with her so much in the last couple of years, somewhat altered my sense of who she was and how I portrayed her in *The Ties That Bind*.

BM: Did other kinds of audiences see *I Cannot Tell You How I Feel*? Are people interested in this film because of their concern with aging?

SF: It's hard to say. I just showed the film in Philadelphia in a series at the Wolf Humanities Center. There were a fair number of people in the audience, and many were older. In other words, they were my age [sixty-four] or older. I didn't know whether they were the people who regularly attended that film series or whether they came because of the subject matter. But there was also a fair number of young people. I think that some people come to see it because they know my work and want to see the new one, and others come because they're dealing with their parents. All my films have attracted a mixed audience, by which I mean that some people come specifically because of the subject matter, and others who come because they know and like my prior work, and they're curious about what I've done next. Consequently, sometimes people in the first group are totally bewildered by the experimental nature of the film, and sometimes people in the second group aren't so keen on the content. But what can you do?

BM: Can you describe current platforms and how distribution works for you now? How was the experience of the retrospective for you?

SF: Distribution is a problem for everybody except for the handful of people who make millions of dollars. For independent fiction and documentary filmmakers, it's a disaster. Most of the audience below the age of thirty thinks everything should be free, and I fear that a lot of older people are also slipping into that frame of mind. Outcast Films distributes almost all of my work; they put out a five-DVD collection of thirteen films a few years ago, and they've added two more titles since then. It's really great for me to have a distributor, but in order to be aligned with the going rate that people are willing to pay, the price for the complete collection of my films is set at $109.

Neither I nor my distributor make very much money when somebody buys a DVD or pays to stream a film, even though she's a good distributor and works hard to make money for the films she represents. It's a serious problem. Many younger filmmakers upload their work to YouTube because they want people to see them and they don't have a distributor so, without hope of making money, why not make it free? At least you get an audience that way. But I don't think anybody should do that. Maybe that sounds unsympathetic. I'm not in their position, and if I were, I might also put things up for free. But it's important for people to realize that we should all be paying for culture, and part of that being made obvious is that artists should insist on being paid for their work. Anyway, I don't put my work on YouTube or Vimeo for free, with the exception of two very short films that aren't in regular distribution. I don't see any reason to try and sell them some other way, so those are on Vimeo.

With all the changes from film prints to DVDs to streaming, I make almost nothing now compared to what I used to make. If I didn't have a teaching job, I wouldn't be able to sustain myself.

BM: Do you see teaching as part of your identity as a filmmaker?

SF: I don't see teaching as part of my identity as a filmmaker in any way except that I teach students how to do the things I do when I'm not teaching. I also don't particularly like the job.

I was hired at Princeton University twenty-two years ago as an adjunct, but after a few years it was turned into a tenured position. Before that I had taught at the New School and at NYU [New York University]. I liked the New School, but they paid nothing. NYU also paid nothing. By nothing, I mean that I was getting around $3,000 total for the semester for a class that ran twelve weeks, or maybe it was fifteen weeks. But however, you do the math, it's nothing. That was in the mid- to late 1990s, and the horrible fact is it's not much different these days for adjunct faculty.

I said before that I don't like the job, but in the same breath I would note that I was really lucky to get the job at Princeton. I've worked as hard as I can to help the students make the best films they can possibly make, even though it's in total conflict with who I am as a filmmaker. I always urge the students to think for themselves and be their own brain and their own heart when they make their films, but they mostly want to learn how to do things "the right way." Obviously, part of my job is to show them how to focus a camera and how to edit sound well. I understand the need to teach them how to do things correctly when it comes to technology, but I have a problem with their desire to say things in the right way as opposed to saying things that they really think and feel.

Most nonteachers think of it as a great gig. You get off three months in the summer, right? But teaching is exhausting, and it cannibalizes your brain. Before I was teaching, I did freelance production work for magazines and books for ten years. It paid really well until the computer arrived. Imagine that in the early 1980s my friends and I were earning between $15 to $25 an hour off the books. So, for ten years, I went to work and did what I was supposed to do, and when I left, I didn't think about it for a single minute until the next time I walked into that work-place, and because it paid so well, we usually only worked for maybe two weeks out of the month. So, my brain was completely free between jobs. But when you teach, you and your time just gets eaten up. I have some friends who teach and who find ways that their teaching informs how they work on their own films, but that's never been my experience.

BM: What is the situation of the aging female artist?

SF: There's the near and the far future. I'm going to retire in the spring of 2023, which is great because then I'll have all the time in the world to do whatever I want. But I've always worked while I've taught, and that's true now and hopefully will be true no matter how much more aging occurs. I just added twenty-six new entries to the website about women editors. I estimate that in a month I will have completed this massive work.

I'm also returning to a project that I started about two years ago, which is a book about a trip that I did through North and West Africa when I was twenty-one years old. It was right after college. I started in Europe, hitchhiked down to Marseilles, took a ferry over to Algiers, got rides on trucks down through the Sahara, and then zig-zagged my way through about seven West African countries. Five months later I flew from Mali to Morocco, took the ferry across to Spain, and then hitchhiked up to Luxembourg to catch a flight back home. I kept a journal and took black and white photographs. When people saw a single, young, white woman with a backpack getting off a truck or a lorry in the marketplace, they were very curious, and someone would usually invite me to stay at their house. I almost never stayed in hotels. I made friends, and many of them wrote me when I was back in New York. I also had correspondence with people back home because this was before the internet. Forty years later, I wondered what was in those journals and those letters, so I spent a summer transcribing all of that material and scanning all the photo negatives. I have a rough draft of the whole thing, but I put it aside while I was creating the *Edited By* website. It will probably take another year or two to finish it. Meanwhile, I'm also collecting images that might be part of the next film I make.

The second issue is about being an older woman artist as opposed to an older male artist, and as we know, being older never seems to matter much if you're a man. In fact, it usually makes people see them as more powerful, experienced, et cetera. When it comes to being an older woman artist, I think we're in a slightly better position these days than we were thirty years ago. There's more respect and some acknowledgment about women being as valuable and productive in their later working life as when they were young. But there's the exhaustion factor. And there's the fear. "Have I run out of ideas?" "Do I have the wherewithal to launch into some new huge project?"

I'm good friends with Yvonne Rainer, and she's exactly twenty years older than me. Whenever I feel as if I might not make another film, I think about what she does. Just recently, she traveled to Scotland and put on three performances. She's so busy, productive, and amazing. She's nowhere near being done working. I hope that's true for me. But one difference is that if I look ahead twenty or thirty years, I think that climate change might change a lot of our circumstances, that we'll be living in a very different, reduced world. I'm not convinced that we're going to reverse this slide, and it's hard to picture where being an artist, being a filmmaker will fit in. That makes me feel lucky that I'm sixty-four years old instead of seven.

1978
Hot Water
United States
Production: Su Friedrich Films
Director, cinematographer, editor: Su Friedrich
12 minutes
Super 8 mm
black and white
available on Vimeo

1979
Cool Hands, Warm Heart
United States
Production: Su Friedrich Films
Distribution: Outcast Films, Canyon Cinema
Director, writer, cinematographer: Su Friedrich
Cast, interview subjects, or voice-over performers: Donna Allegra Simms, Sally
    Eckhoff, Jennifer MacDonald, Rose Maurer, Marty Pottenger
16 minutes
Super 8 mm and 16 mm
black and white

1979
Scar Tissue
United States
Production: Su Friedrich Films
Distribution: Outcast Films, Canyon Cinema
Director, cinematographer, editor: Su Friedrich
6 minutes
Super 8 mm and 16 mm
black and white

1980
I Suggest Mine
United States
Production: Su Friedrich Films
Distribution: Private Collection
Director, cinematographer, editor: Su Friedrich
6 minutes
16 mm
color and black and white
private collection of Su Friedrich

1981
Gently Down the Stream
United States
Production: Su Friedrich Films
Distribution: Outcast Films, Canyon Cinema, The Film-Makers' Cooperative, Canadian Filmmakers Distribution Centre, Freunde der Deutschen Kinemathek, Light Cone
Director, writer, cinematographer, editor: Su Friedrich
Cast, interview subjects, or voice-over performers: Jennifer MacDonald, Marty Pottenger
14 minutes
Super 8 mm and 16 mm
black and white

1982
But No One
United States
Production: Su Friedrich Films
Distribution: Outcast Films, Canyon Cinema
Director, writer, cinematographer, editor: Su Friedrich
9 minutes
16 mm
black and white
Funding: New York State Council on the Arts

1984
The Ties That Bind
United States
Production: Su Friedrich Films
Distribution: Outcast Films, Canyon Cinema, Canadian Filmmakers Distribution Centre, Freunde der Deutschen Kinemathek, Light Cone
Director, writer, cinematographer, editor, sound editor: Su Friedrich

Cast, interview subject, or voice-over performer: Lore Friedrich
55 minutes
16 mm
black and white
Funding: New York State Council on the Arts

1987
Damned If You Don't
United States
Production: Su Friedrich Films
Distribution: Outcast Films, Canyon Cinema, The Film-Makers' Cooperative, Canadian Filmmakers Distribution Centre, Freunde der Deutschen Kinemathek, Light Cone
Director, writer, cinematographer, editor, sound editor: Su Friedrich
Script consultant: Cathy Nan Quinlan
Cast, interview subjects, or voice-over performers: Peggy Healey, Makea McDonald, Cathy Nan Quinlan, Martina Siebert, Ela Troyano
42 minutes
16 mm
black and white
Funding: New York State Council on the Arts, Jerome Foundation, German Academic Exchange Service

1990
Sink or Swim
United States
Production: Su Friedrich Films
Distribution: Outcast Films, Canyon Cinema, Canadian Filmmakers Distribution Centre, Freunde der Deutschen Kinemathek, Light Cone
Director, writer, cinematographer, editor, sound editor: Su Friedrich
Additional Cinematographers: Peggy Ahwesh, Carl J. Friedrich
Cast, interview subjects, or voice-over performers: Jessica Lynn, Martina Meijer, Peggy Ahwesh
48 minutes
16 mm
Black and white
Funding: Guggenheim Foundation, New York State Council on the Arts, Jerome Foundation, New York Foundation on the Arts, Art Matters Inc.

1991
First Comes Love
United States
Production: Jezebel Productions Inc.

Distribution: Outcast Films, Canyon Cinema, The Film-Makers' Cooperative, Canadian Filmmakers Distribution Centre, Freunde der Deutschen Kinemathek
Director, writer, cinematographer, editor, sound editor: Su Friedrich
22 minutes
16 mm
black and white
Funding: The Rockefeller Foundation

1993
Lesbian Avengers Eat Fire, Too
United States
Production: The Lesbian Avengers
Distribution: Outcast Films, The Lesbian Avengers
Directors, writers, editors, sound editors: Janet Baus, Su Friedrich
Cinematographers: Janet Baus, Jean Carlomusto, Julie Clark, Su Friedrich, Harriet Hirschorn
60 minutes
video
color

1993
Rules of the Road
United States
Production: Jezebel Productions Inc.
Distribution: Outcast Films, Canyon Cinema, Canadian Filmmakers Distribution Centre, Freunde der Deutschen Kinemathek, Light Cone
Director, writer, cinematographer, editor, sound editor: Su Friedrich
31 minutes
16 mm
color
Funding: The Rockefeller Foundation

1996
Hide and Seek
United States
Production: Downstream Productions Inc.
Producers: Eva Kolodner, Katie Roumel
Distribution: Outcast Films, Canyon Cinema, Freunde der Deutschen Kinemathek
Executive producer, director, editor: Su Friedrich
Writers: Su Friedrich, Cathy Nan Quinlan

Cinematographers: Jim Denault, Su Friedrich
Editing consultant: Cathy Nan Quinlan
Sound editor: Juan Carlos Martinez
Cast, interview subjects, or voice-over performers: Mindy Baransky, Cindy Bink, Ashley Carlisle, Gina Caulfield, Kelly Cogswell, Marlene Colburn, Dorothy Donaher, Ashley Ferrante, Tracey Frederick, Su Friedrich, Virginia Gravli, Chelsea Holland, Marie Honan, Delritta Hornbuckle, Hunter Johnson, Alisa Lebow, Alicia Manta, Ariel Mara, Nikki Michaels, Kirsten Oriol, Lydia Pacifico, Matthew Pavlov, Jane Perkins, Cheryl Perry, Ann Podolske, Pat Powell, Frank Rosner, Linda Small, Sarah Jane Smith, Claudia Steinberg, Linzy Taylor, Brandon Winston, Maleena Waddy, Jean Edna White, Noah Wilson, Penny Wright, Apryl Wynter
65 minutes
16 mm
black and white
Funding: Independent Television Service, National Endowment for the Arts, New York State Council on the Arts

2002
The Odds of Recovery
United States
Production: Downstream Productions Inc.
Distribution: Outcast Films, Canyon Cinema
Director, writer, cinematographer, editor, sound editor: Su Friedrich
Additional cinematographer: Joel Schlemowitz
65 minutes
16 mm and video
color
Funding: New York State Council on the Arts, New York Foundation of the Arts, Charette Communications

2004
The Head of a Pin
United States
Production: Downstream Productions Inc.
Distribution: Outcast Films
Director, cinematographer, editor, sound editor: Su Friedrich
Cast, interview subjects, or voice-over performers: Barbara Epler, Cathy Nan Quinlan, Claudia Steinberg
21 minutes
video
color

2005
Seeing Red
United States
Production: Downstream Productions Inc.
Distribution: Outcast Films
Director, cinematographer, editor, sound editor: Su Friedrich
27 minutes
video
color

2008
From the Ground Up
United States
Production: Su Friedrich Films
Distribution: Su Friedrich Films
Director, writer, cinematographer, editor, sound editor: Su Friedrich
Additional cinematographer: Pedro Díaz Valdés
Music: Kurt Hoffman and Meg Richardt
54 minutes
video
color
Funding: New York State Council on the Arts

2012
Practice Makes Perfect
United States
Production: Su Friedrich Films
Director, cinematographer, editor, sound editor: Su Friedrich
Cast, interview subject, or voice-over performer: Kam Kelly
11 minutes
video
color
Available on Vimeo
Commission: BAM (Brooklyn Academy of Music)

2012
Gut Renovation
United States
Production: Su Friedrich Films
Distribution: Outcast Films
Director, writer, cinematographer, editor, sound editor: Su Friedrich
Cowriter and editing consultant: Cathy Nan Quinlan

81 minutes
video
color

2013
Queen Takes Pawn
United States
Production: Su Friedrich Films
Director, editor, sound editor: Su Friedrich
Cinematographers: Su Friedrich, Carl J. Friedrich
6.5 minutes
video
color and black and white
available on Vimeo

2016
I Cannot Tell You How I Feel
United States
Production: Su Friedrich Films
Distribution: Icarus Films
Director, writer, cinematographer, editor, sound editor: Su Friedrich
Cowriter: Cathy Nan Quinlan
Cast, interview subjects, or voice-over performers: Lore Friedrich, Maria Friedrich, Pete Friedrich
42 minutes
video
color and black and white

2020
5/10/20
United States
Production: Su Friedrich Films
Director, cinematographer, editor, sound editor: Su Friedrich
2 minutes
video
color
available on Vimeo (as a single film) and as part of the Cinetracts '20 project
    at www.wexarts.org
Commission: Wexner Center for the Arts Artist Residency Award, Ohio State
    University (as part of the Cinetracts '20 project)

Ahmed, Sara. *The Cultural Politics of Emotion*. New York: Routledge, 2004.
———. *Living a Feminist Life*. Durham, NC: Duke University Press, 2017.
Ahwesh, Peggy, Caroline Avery, Craig Baldwin, Abigail Child, Su Friedrich, Barbara Hammer, Todd Haynes, Lewis Klar, Ross McLaren, John Porter, Yvonne Rainer, Berenice Reynaud, Keith Sanborn, Sarah Schulman, Jeffrey Skoller, Phil Solomon, and Leslie Thornton, and fifty-nine other filmmakers. "Open Letter to the Experimental Film Congress: Let's Set the Record Straight" (Canada, 1989). In *Film Manifestos and Global Cinema Cultures: A Critical Anthology*, edited by Scott MacKenzie, 100–101. Berkeley: University of California Press, 2014.
Bad Object-Choices, ed. *How Do I Look: Queer Film and Video*. Seattle: Bay Press, 1991.
Baer, Hester, and Angelica Fenner. "Introduction: Revisiting Feminism and German Cinema." *Camera Obscura* 99 (2018): 1–20.
Baer, Nicholas, Maggie Hennefeld, Laura Horak, and Gunnar Iversen, eds. *Unwatchable*. New Brunswick, NJ: Rutgers University Press, 2019.
Baracco, Alberto. *Philosophy in Stan Brakhage's "Dog Star Man": World, Metaphor, Interpretation*. London, England: Palgrave Pivot, 2019.
Barbanel, Josh. "Under 'Rainbow,' a War: When Politics, Morals and Learning Mix." *New York Times*, December 27, 1992, sec. 1, 34, https://www.nytimes.com/, accessed June 28, 2020.
Barker, Jennifer M. *The Tactile Eye: Touch and the Cinematic Experience*. Berkeley: University of California Press, 2009.
Baron, Jaimie. "The Archive Effect: Archival Footage as an Experience of Reception." *Projections* 6.2 (2012): 102–20.
Bazin, André. "De la Politique des Auteurs (1957)." In *Auteurs and Authorship: A Film Reader*, edited by Barry Keith Grant, 19–28. Malden, MA: Blackwell, 2008.
Berlant, Lauren, and Michael Warner. "Sex in Public." *Critical Inquiry* 24.2 (1998): 547–66.
Berler, Caroline. "Interview for *Dykes, Camera, Action!*" (2016) In *Su Friedrich: Interviews*, edited by Sonia Misra and Rox Samer, 104–15. Jackson: University Press of Mississippi, 2022.

Bessette, Jean. *Retroactivism in the Lesbian Archives: Composing Pasts and Futures*. Carbondale: Southern Illinois University Press, 2018.

Beugnet, Martine. *Cinema and Sensation: French Film and the Art of Transgression*. Edinburgh: Edinburgh University Press, 2007. Kindle.

Blaetz, Robin, ed. *Women's Experimental Cinema: Critical Frameworks*. Durham, NC: Duke University Press, 2007.

Bociurkiw, Marusya. "Big Affect: The Ephemeral Archive of Second-Wave Feminist Video Collectives in Canada." *Camera Obscura* 93 (2016): 5–33.

Bolter, Jay David, and Richard Grusin. *Remediation: Understanding New Media*. Cambridge, MA: MIT Press, 2000.

Bradbury-Rance, Clara. *Lesbian Cinema after Queer Theory*. Edinburgh: Edinburgh University Press, 2019.

Brakhage, Stan. *Essential Brakhage: Selected Writings on Film-Making*. Kingston, NY: McPherson, 2001.

———. *Film Biographies: Stan Brakhage*. Berkeley, CA: Turtle Island Foundation, 1977.

———. *Stan Brakhage: Metaphors on Vision*. New York City: Anthology Film Archives, 2017.

———. *Telling Time: Essays of a Visionary Filmmaker*. Kingston, NY: McPherson, 2018.

Brown, Judith C. *Immodest Acts: The Life of a Lesbian Nun in Renaissance Italy*. New York: Oxford University Press, 1986.

Bruhm, Steven, and Natasha Hurley, eds. *Curiouser: On the Queerness of Children*. Minneapolis: University of Minnesota Press, 2004.

Brunow, Dagmar. *Remediating Transcultural Memory: Documentary Filmmaking as Archival Intervention*. Berlin: De Gruyter, 2015.

Butler, Judith. *Gender Trouble: Feminism and the Subversion of Identity*. New York: Routledge, 1990. Kindle.

Cabañas, Kaira M. *Off-Screen Cinema: Isidore Isou and the Lettrist Avant-Garde*. Chicago: University of Chicago Press, 2014.

Camera Obscura Collective. "Collectivity: Part 1." *Camera Obscura* 91 (2016): 1–2.

Camera Obscura Collective. "Collectivity: Part 2." *Camera Obscura* 93 (2016): 1–2.

Camia, Giovanni Marchini. "Su Friedrich in the Swamp of Images." (2016). In *Su Friedrich: Interviews*, edited by Sonia Misra and Rox Samer, 99–103. Jackson: University Press of Mississippi, 2022.

Carr, Cynthia, Betsy Crowell, Betsy Damon, Rose Fichtenholtz, Louise Fishman, Su Friedrich, Harmony Hammond, Marty Pottenger, Amy Sillman, Christine Wade, Kathy Webster (Third Issue Collective). "Lesbian Arts and Artists." *Heresies: A Feminist Publication on Art and Politics* 3 (1977). http://heresiesfilmproject.org/, accessed June 25, 2020.

Cogswell, Kelly. *Eating Fire: My Life as a Lesbian Avenger*. Minneapolis: University of Minnesota Press, 2014.

Colangelo, Dave. *The Building as Screen: A History, Theory, and Practice of Massive Media*. Amsterdam: Amsterdam University Press, 2020.

Columpar, Corinn. "A Permeable Practice: *Shortbus* and the Politics of Cinematic Collaboration." *Camera Obscura* 91 (2016): 5–25.

Curb, Rosemary Keefe. "What Is a Lesbian Nun?" In *Lesbian Nuns: Breaking Silence* (1985), edited by Nancy Manahan and Rosemary Keefe Curb, location 388–569. Midway, FL: Spinsters, 2013. Kindle.

Cutler, Janet. "Su Friedrich: Breaking the Rules." In *Women's Experimental Cinema: Critical Frameworks*, edited by Robin Blaetz, 312–38. Durham, NC: Duke University Press, 2007.

Cvetkovich, Ann. *An Archive of Feelings: Trauma, Sexuality and Lesbian Public Cultures*. Durham, NC: Duke University Press, 2003.

———. "The Artist as Archivist, the Archive as Art." In *Barbara Hammer: Evidentiary Bodies*, edited by Staci Bu Shea and Carmel Curtis, 39–42. Munich: Hirmer, 2018.

Delardi, Cayla. "CALA Staff Member Anne Maguire Discusses Barbara Hammer's History Lessons at Whitney Museum Screening." *New York University*, August 2, 2019. Accessed June 28, 2020. https://wpqa.nyu.edu/sps-cala/2019/08/02/cala-staff-member-anne-maguire-discusses-barbara-hammers-history-lessons-at-whitney-museum-screening/.

de Lauretis, Teresa. "Film and the Visible." In *How Do I Look: Queer Film and Video*, edited by Bad Object-Choices, 223–64. Seattle: Bay Press, 1991.

Deleuze, Gilles, and Félix Guattari. *Kafka: Toward a Minor Literature*. Minneapolis: University of Minnesota Press, 1986.

Di Liscia, Valentina. "Who Owns the Logo of the Lesbian Avengers, Decades Later?" *Hyperallergic*, June 25, 2021. Accessed September 6, 2021. https://hyperallergic.com/.

Dixon, Wheeler Winston, and Gwendolyn Audrey Foster, eds. *Experimental Cinema: The Film Reader*. London: Routledge, 2002.

Dyer, Richard. *Now You See It: Studies on Lesbian and Gay Film*. New York: Routledge, 1990.

Edited By: Women Film Editors. Created by Su Friedrich. Accessed August 2, 2020. http://womenfilmeditors.princeton.edu/.

Eisner, Lotte H. *The Haunted Screen: Expressionism in German Cinema and the Influence of Max Reinhart*. 1952. Berkeley: University of California Press, 2008.

Fischer, Lucy. *Cinematernity: Film, Motherhood, Genre*. Princeton, NJ: Princeton University Press, 1996.

Frampton, Hollis. *Circles of Confusion: Film, Photography, Video: Texts 1968–1980*. Rochester, NY: Visual Studies Workshop Press, 1983.

———. *On the Camera Arts and Consecutive Matters: The Writings of Hollis Frampton*. Cambridge, MA: MIT Press, 2009.

Freeman, Elizabeth. *The Wedding Complex: Forms of Belonging in Modern American Culture*. Durham, NC: Duke University Press, 2002.

Friedan, Betty. *The Feminine Mystique*. 1963. New York: Norton, 1997.

Friedrich, Su. "Letters." *The Downtown Review* 2.1 (1979–80): 42–43.

———. "Mea Culpa." Special volume, Patterns of Communication and Space among Women. *Heresies* 1.2 (1977): 26–29.

———. "Radical Form: Radical Content." *Millennium Film Journal* 22 (1989–90): 118–23.

Fujiwara, Chris. "Convent Erotica." *Hermenaut 14*, July 19, 1998/99. https://web.archive.org/web/20110719183028/http://www.hermenaut.com/a48.shtml. Accessed June 25, 2020.

Gaines, Jane M., and Michael Renov, eds. *Collecting Visible Evidence*. Minneapolis: University of Minnesota Press, 1999.

Galm, Ruth. "The Millennium Film Workshop in Love." In *Captured: A Film/Video History of the Lower East Side*, edited by Clayton Patterson, 101–4. New York: Seven Stories Press, 2005.

Galt, Rosalind. *Pretty: Film and the Decorative Image*. New York: Columbia University Press, 2011.

Ganguly, Suranjan. *Stan Brakhage: Interviews*. Jackson: University Press of Mississippi, 2017.

Geiger, Jeffrey. "Intimate Media: New Queer Documentary and the Sensory Turn." *Studies in Documentary Film* 14.3 (2020): 177–201.

Gever, Martha, John Greyson, and Pratibha Parmar, eds. *Queer Looks: Perspectives on Gay and Lesbian Film and Video*. London: Routledge, 1993.

Goethe, Johann Wolfgang von. *Faust: A Tragedy*. Translated by Walter Arndt. New York: Norton, 1998.

Gorfinkel, Elena. *Lewd Looks: American Sexploitation Cinema in the 1960s*. Minneapolis: University of Minnesota Press, 2017.

Gunning, Tom. "The Cinema of Attractions: Early Film, Its Spectator and the Avant-Garde." In *Early Cinema: Space, Frame, Narrative*, edited by Thomas Elsaesser, 56–62. London: British Film Institute, 1990.

———. "Towards a Minor Cinema: Fonoroff, Herwitz, Ahwesh, Lapore, Klahr, Solomon." *Motion Picture* 3.1–2 (1989–90): 2–5.

Halberstam, Jack. *Female Masculinity*. Durham, NC: Duke University Press, 1998.

———. *In a Queer Time and Place: Transgender Bodies, Subcultural Lives*. New York: New York University Press, 2005.

———. "Oh Bondage Up Yours? Female Masculinity and the Tomboy." In *Curiouser: On the Queerness of Children*, edited by Steven Bruhm and Natasha Hurley, 191–214. Minneapolis: University of Minnesota Press, 2004.

———. *The Queer Art of Failure*. Durham, NC: Duke University Press, 2011. Kindle.

Hanisch, Carol. "The Personal Is Political." In *Radical Feminism: A Documentary Reader*, edited by Barbara A. Crow, 113–16. New York: New York University Press, 2000.

Hanlon, Lindley. "Female Rage: The Films of Su Friedrich." *Millennium Film Journal* 12 (1983): 78–86.

Heartney, Eleanor, Helaine Posner, Nancy Princenthal, and Sue Scott. "Introduction." In *After the Revolution: Women Who Transformed Contemporary Art*, edited by Heartney, Eleanor, Helaine Posner, Nancy Princenthal, and Sue Scott, 9–27. New York: Prestel, 2007.

Hilderbrand, Lucas. "Retroactivism." *GLQ: A Journal of Lesbian and Gay Studies* 12.2 (2006): 303–17.

Hirsch, Marianne. *Family Frames: Photography, Narrative, and Postmemory.* Cambridge, MA: Harvard University Press, 1997.

Holmlund, Chris. "Feminist Makeovers: The Celluloid Surgery of Valie Export and Su Friedrich." In *Play It Again, Sam: Retakes on Remakes*, edited by Andrew Horton and Stuart Y. McDougal, 217–37. Oakland: University of California Press, 1998.

———. "The Films of Sadie Benning and Su Friedrich." In *Experimental Cinema: The Film Reader*, edited by Wheeler Winston Dixon and Gwendolyn Audrey Foster, 299–312. London: Routledge, 2002.

———. "When Autobiography Meets Ethnography and Girl Meets Girl: The 'Dyke Docs' of Sadie Benning and Su Friedrich." In *Between the Sheets, in the Streets: Queer, Lesbian, Gay Documentary*, edited by Chris Holmlund and Cynthia Fuchs, 127–43. Minneapolis: University of Minnesota Press, 1997.

Ivanchikova, Alla. "Machinic Intimacies and Mechanical Brides: Collectivity between Prosthesis and Surrogacy in Jonathan Mostow's *Surrogates* and Spike Jonze's *Her.*" *Camera Obscura* 91 (2016): 65–91.

James, David. *Stan Brakhage: Filmmaker.* Philadelphia: Temple University Press, 2011.

Juhasz, Alexandra. "'They said we were trying to show reality—all I want to show is my video': The Politics of the Realist Feminist Documentary." *Screen* 35.2 (1994): 171–90.

Kael, Pauline. "Circles and Squares" (excerpt, 1963). In *Auteurs and Authorship: A Film Reader*, edited by Barry Keith Grant, 46–54. Malden, MA: Blackwell, 2008.

Keller, Sarah. *Barbara Hammer: Pushing Out of the Frame.* Detroit: Wayne State University Press, 2021.

Koponen, Sandra. "The 60s; Notes on the Underground." In *Captured: A Film/Video History of the Lower East Side*, edited by Clayton Patterson, 113–20. New York: Seven Stories Press, 2005.

Kotz, Liz. "An Unrequited Desire for the Sublime: Looking at Lesbian Representation across the Works of Abigail Child, Cecilia Doughterty, and Su Friedrich." In *Queer Looks: Perspectives on Gay and Lesbian Film and Video*, edited by Martha Gever, John Greyson, and Pratibha Parmar, 86–102. London: Routledge, 1993.

Kuhn, Annette. *Family Secrets: Acts of Memory and Imagination.* London: Verso, 1995.

Kyröla, Katariina. "Squirming in the Classroom: *Fat Girl* and the Ethical Value of Extreme Discomfort." In *Unwatchable*, edited by Nicholas Baer, Maggie

Hennefeld, Laura Horak, and Gunnar Iversen, 317–21. New Brunswick: Rutgers University Press, 2019. Kindle.

Landsberg, Alison. *Prosthetic Memory: The Transformation of American Remembrance in the Age of Mass Culture*. New York: Columbia University Press, 2004.

Lewis, Jon, ed. *The New American Cinema*. Durham, NC: Duke University Press, 1998.

Lori, Marco, and Esther Leslie. *Stan Brakhage: The Realm Buster*. East Barnett, England: John Libbey, 2018.

Lugo, Cynthia. "It's Alright, Williamsburg (I'm Only Bleeding)." In *Su Friedrich: Interviews*, edited by Sonia Misra and Rox Samer, 73–76. Jackson: University Press of Mississippi, 2022.

MacDonald, Scott. "Daddy Dearest: Su Friedrich Talks about Filmmaking, Family, and Feminism." *The Independent* (1990): 28–34.

———. "Damned If You Don't: An Interview with Su Friedrich." *Afterimage* 15 (1988): 6–10.

———. "From Zygote to Global Cinema via Su Friedrich's Films." *Journal of Film and Video* 44.1–2 (1992): 30–41.

———. "Su Friedrich." In *A Critical Cinema 2: Interviews with Independent Filmmakers*, by Scott MacDonald, 283–318. Berkeley: University of California Press, 1992.

———. "Su Friedrich: *The Ties That Bind*." In *Avant-Garde Film: Motion Studies*, by Scott MacDonald, 102–11. Cambridge: Cambridge University Press, 1993.

Manahan, Nancy, and Rosemary Keefe Curb, eds. *Lesbian Nuns: Breaking Silence*. (1985) Midway, FL: Spinsters, 2013.

Marks, Laura U. *The Skin of the Film: Intercultural Cinema, Embodiment, and the Senses*. Durham, NC: Duke University Press, 2000.

Martin, Katy. "Su Friedrich." In *Su Friedrich: Interviews*, edited by Sonia Misra and Rox Samer, 62–72. Jackson: University Press of Mississippi, 2022.

Mayne, Judith. "Su Friedrich's Swimming Lessons." In *Framed: Lesbians, Feminists, and Media Culture*, by Judith Mayne, 193–211. Minneapolis: University of Minnesota Press, 2000.

McKinney, Cait. *Information Activism: A Queer History of Lesbian Media Technologies*. Durham, NC: Duke University Press, 2020.

Mekas, Jonas. *A Dance with Fred Astaire*. New York City: Anthology Editions, 2017.

———. "A Few Notes on My Life on the Lower East Side & Cinema." In *Captured: A Film/Video History of the Lower East Side*, edited by Clayton Patterson, 97–100. New York: Seven Stories Press, 2005.

———. *I Had Nowhere to Go*. Leipzig, Germany: Spector Books, 2017.

———. *Jonas Mekas: Just Like a Shadow*. Göttingen, Germany: Steidl, 2000.

———. *Movie Journal: The Rise of the New American Cinema, 1959–1971*. New York: Columbia University Press, 2016.

———. *Words Apart and Others*. Brooklyn: Rail Editions, 2019.

Mellencamp, Patricia. *Indiscretions: Avant-Garde Film, Video, & Feminism*. Bloomington: Indiana University Press, 1990.

Menne, Jeff. "The Last Qualitative Scientist: Hollis Frampton and the Digital Arts Lab." In *In the Studio: Visual Creation and Its Material Environments*, edited by Brian R. Jacobson, 4806–5249. Oakland: University of California Press, 2020. Kindle.

Meyerling, Max von. "The Lower East Side on Film." In *Captured: A Film/Video History of the Lower East Side*, edited by Clayton Patterson, 107–12. New York: Seven Stories Press, 2005.

Misra, Sonia, and Rox Samer. "Introduction." In *Su Friedrich: Interviews*, edited by Sonia Misra and Rox Samer, vii–xii. Jackson: University Press of Mississippi, 2022.

Moore, Rachel. *Hollis Frampton: (nostalgia)*. Cambridge, MA: MIT Press, 2006.

Moskowitz, Peter E. *How to Kill a City: Gentrification, Inequality, and the Fight for the Neighborhood*. New York: Bold Type, 2017.

Muhlstein, Cecilia. "Su Friedrich's Cinema." In *Su Friedrich: Interviews*, edited by Sonia Misra and Rox Samer, 58–61. Jackson: University Press of Mississippi, 2022.

Mulvey, Laura. "Visual Pleasure and Narrative Cinema." (1975) In *Feminism and Film Theory*, edited by Constance Penley, 57–68. New York: Routledge, 1988.

Murray, Ros. "Raised Fists: Politics, Technology, and Embodiment in 1970s French Feminist Video Collectives." *Camera Obscura* 91 (2016): 93–121.

Ngai, Sianne. *Ugly Feelings*. Cambridge, MA: Harvard University Press, 2005.

Nichols, Bill. *Introduction to Documentary*. Bloomington: Indiana University Press, 2010.

Organizers, The. "Statement by the Organizers: The Second New York Lesbian and Gay Experimental Film Festival. Radical Form: Radical Content." *Millennium Film Journal* 22 (1989–90): 117.

Orgeron, Devin, Marsha Orgeron, and Dan Streible, eds. *Learning with the Lights Off: Educational Film in the United States*. Oxford: Oxford University Press, 2012.

Osterweil, Ara. *Flesh Cinema: The Corporeal Turn in American Avant-Garde Film*. Manchester, England: Manchester University Press, 2014.

Passet, Joanne E. Foreword. "Lesbians Nuns: Breaking Silence, Revered and Reviled." In *Lesbian Nuns: Breaking Silence* (1985), edited by Nancy Manahan and Rosemary Keefe Curb, location 110–374. Midway, FL: Spinsters, 2013. Kindle.

Petrolle, Jean, and Virginia Wright Wexman. "Introduction: Experimental Filmmaking and Women's Subjectivity." In *Women & Experimental Filmmaking*, edited by Jean Petrolle and Virgina Wright Wexman, 1–18. Urbana: University of Illinois Press, 2005.

Phelan, Peggy. "Survey." In *Art and Feminism*, edited by Helena Reckitt, 14–49. New York: Phaidon, 2001.

"Renegades: Butches and Studs, in Their Own Words." *New York Times Style Magazine*, April 2020. Accessed August 1, 2020. https://www.nytimes.com.

Renov, Michael. "Domestic Ethnography and the Construction of the 'Other' Self." In *Collecting Visible Evidence*, edited by Jane M. Gaines and Michael Renov, 140–55. Minneapolis: University of Minnesota Press, 1999.

———. "New Subjectivities: Documentary and Self-Representation." In *Feminism and Documentary*, edited by Diane Waldman and Janet Walker, 84–94. Minneapolis: University of Minnesota Press, 1999.

———. *The Subject of Documentary*. Minneapolis: University of Minnesota Press, 2004.

Rich, Ruby B. *Chick Flicks: Theories and Memories of the Feminist Film Movement*. Durham, NC: Duke University Press, 1998.

———. "New Queer Cinema." 1992. In *New Queer Cinema: A Critical Reader*, edited by Michele Aaron, 15–22. Edinburgh: Edinburgh University Press, 2004.

Roth, Moira, ed. *The Amazing Decade: Women and Performance Art in America 1970–1980*. Los Angeles: Astro Artz, 1983.

Rothberg, Michael. *The Implicated Subject: Beyond Victims and Perpetrators*. Stanford, CA: Stanford University Press, 2019.

———. *Multidirectional Memory: Remembering the Holocaust in the Age of Decolonization*. Stanford, CA: Stanford University Press, 2009.

Russell, Catherine. "Culture as Fiction: The Ethnographic Impulse in the Films of Peggy Ahwesh, Su Friedrich, and Leslie Thornton." In *The New American Cinema*, edited by Jon Lewis, 353–78. Durham, NC: Duke University Press, 1998.

———. *Experimental Ethnography: The Work of Film in the Age of Video*. Durham, NC: Duke University Press, 1999.

Salamon, Gayle. *Assuming a Body: Transgender and Rhetorics of Materiality*. New York: Columbia University Press, 2010.

Samer, Rox. *Lesbian Potentiality & Feminist Media in the 1970s*. Durham, NC: Duke University Press, 2022.

Sarris, Andrew. "Notes on the Auteur Theory in 1962." In *Auteurs and Authorship: A Film Reader*, edited by Barry Keith Grant, 35–45. Malden, MA: Blackwell, 2008.

Schneider, Rebecca. *The Explicit Body in Performance*. New York City: Routledge, 1997.

Sedgwick, Eve Kosofsky. "How to Bring Your Kids Up Gay: The War on Effeminate Boys." In *Curiouser: On the Queerness of Children*, edited by Steven Bruhm and Natasha Hurley, 139–49. Minneapolis: University of Minnesota Press, 2004.

Segura, Carlos. J. "Q&A with Filmmaker Su Friedrich." (2013) In *Su Friedrich: Interviews*, edited by Sonia Misra and Rox Samer, 77–79. Jackson: University Press of Mississippi, 2022.

Sempel, Peter. "Jonas Mekas." In *Captured: A Film/Video History of the Lower East Side*, edited by Clayton Patterson, 89–96. New York: Seven Stories Press, 2005.

Siegel, Carol. "Compulsory Heterophobia: The Aesthetics of Seriousness and the Production of Homophobia." In *Forming and Reforming Identity*, edited by Carol Siegel and Ann Kibbey, 319–38. New York: New York University Press, 1995.

Sitney, P. Adams. *Visionary Film: The American Avant-Garde, 1943–2000*. 3rd ed. Oxford: Oxford University Press, 2002.

Sobchack, Vivian. *Carnal Thoughts: Embodiment and Moving Image Culture*. Berkeley: University of California Press, 2004.

Staiger, Janet. "Authorship Approaches." In *Authorship and Film*, edited by David A. Gerstner and Janet Staiger, 27–57. London: Routledge, 2003.

Steinberg, Claudia. "Su Friedrich." In *Su Friedrich: Interviews*, edited by Sonia Misra and Rox Samer, 80–88. Jackson: University Press of Mississippi, 2022.

Stockton, Kathryn Bond. *The Queer Child or Growing Sideways in the Twentieth Century*. Durham, NC: Duke University Press, 2009.

Straayer, Chris. *Deviant Eyes, Deviant Bodies: Sexual Re-Orientations in Film and Video*. New York: Columbia University Press, 1996.

Street, Sarah. *Black Narcissus*. London: I.B. Taurus, 2005.

The 'temporary Museum of Painting (& drawing). Accessed June 25, 2020. http://thetemporarymuseum.com/index.htm.

Thürmer-Rohr, Christina. *Vagabonding: Feminist Thinking Cut Loose*. Translated by Lise Weil. Boston: Beacon, 1991.

Waldman, Diane, and Janet Walker, eds. *Feminism and Documentary*. Minneapolis: University of Minnesota Press, 1999.

Wall-Romana, Christophe. "Unwatchability by Choice: Isou's *Venom and Eternity*." In *Unwatchable*, edited by Nicholas Baer, Maggie Hennefeld, Laura Horak, and Gunnar Iversen, 172–77. New Brunswick, NJ: Rutgers University Press, 2019.

Wark, Jayne. *Radical Gestures: Feminism and Performance Art in North America*. Montreal: McGill-Queen's University Press, 2006.

Warner, Michael. *Publics and Counterpublics*. New York: Zone Books, 2005.

Waugh, Thomas. *The Right to Play Oneself: Looking Back on Documentary Film*. Minneapolis: University of Minnesota Press, 2011.

Wees, William C. "No More Giants." In *Women & Experimental Filmmaking*, edited by Jean Petrolle and Virginia Wright Wexman, 22–43. Urbana: University of Illinois Press, 2005.

Weiss, Andrea. *Vampires and Violets: Lesbians in Film*. New York: Penguin, 1992.

White, Jerry. *Stan Brakhage in Rolling Stock, 1980–1990*. Waterloo, Canada: Wilfrid Laurier University Press, 2018.

Wodening, Jane. *Brakhage's Childhood*. New York: Granary Books, 2015.

Youmans, Greg. "Beyond Cultural Feminism: New Approaches to Barbara Hammer's Early Films." In *Barbara Hammer: Evidentiary Bodies*, edited by Staci Bu Shea and Carmel Curtis, 79–81. Munich: Hirmer, 2018.

———. "Performing Essentialism: Reassessing Barbara Hammer's Films of the 1970s." *Camera Obscura* 81 (2012): 101–36.

———. "'Thank you Anita!': Gay and Lesbian Activist and Experimental Filmmaking of the Late 1970s." Diss., University of California, Santa Cruz, 2009.

Youngblood, Gene. *Expanded Cinema*. New York: Dutton, 1970.

Friedrich, Lore Bucher: husband's abandonment of family and remarriages, 8–9, 69, 70, 72–77; immigration from Germany, 55, 69, 76; life in Nazi Germany, 8, 12–13, 15–16, 55–59, 137, 145; meets and marries SF father, Paul, 8, 55, 69; moves closer to children, 115–16. See also *I Cannot Tell You How I Feel*; *The Ties That Bind*

Friedrich, Maria, 69

Friedrich, Paul Wilhelm: abandonment of family and remarriages, 8–9, 69, 70, 72–77; career as linguistic anthropologist, 8–9, 55, 69, 71, 74–75, 138; death of teenaged sister, 70, 71–72; meets and marries SF mother, Lore, 8, 55, 69; narcissistic personality, 69–75; post–World War II service, 8, 55, 69; travel to Mexico, 69, 74; at the University of Chicago, 9, 69; at the University of Pennsylvania, 69; at Yale University, 8, 69. See also *Sink or Swim*

Friedrich, Su (SF), biographical information: arrival in New York City, 10, 21, 23, 121–22; birth in New Haven, Connecticut, 8, 9; book about travels in Africa, 148; early education, 70; education at Oberlin College, 9, 21, 121, 123; education at the University of Chicago, 9; family background, 8–9, 69, 70, 72–77, 124, 130, 138, 140, 145 (*see also* Friedrich, Lore Bucher; Friedrich, Paul Wilhelm); Maria Friedrich, 69; *Heresies* collective and, 21, 26, 30, 119n7, 123; kinship model of family and, 74–75, 75, 76; membership in the Lesbian Avengers, 14, 142; personal alternative lifestyles, 14, 91–94, 107–8, 110–15; photography/photography studies, 9, 12, 21–22, 58, 121–22, 131, 148; radical lesbian politics and, 7, 77–80, 84; as second-wave feminist, 1, 9, 117 (*see also* second-wave feminism); trip to Mexico with father, 74

Friedrich, Su, filmmaking of: artisanal projects and, 2–3, 105–7, 140; artist residency in West Berlin, 62; awards and honors (*see* awards and honors of SF); biographical information and (*see* Friedrich, Su (SF), biographical information); Catholicism and (*see* Christianity); commitment to collaborative work, 4–6, 20–21, 125, 126, 141–44; DVD collection, 18, 146; editing process (*see* editing process); expanded auteurism/signature style and, 1–7, 91, 102–3, 117–18; as an experimental/documentary filmmaker, 123; feminism/feminist film theory and, 123–24, 126; filmmaker travel with films and, 128–30; filmmaking process (*see* filmmaking process); film mentors of SF, 121–23, 127, 129, 134; films as form media archeology and, 76–77, 109–10; films made for hire, 18–19; film titles and, 15–17; fitness/bodybuilding shots, 43–44, 70, 130; freelance production work and, 147; funding issues and, 62, 94–95, 102, 123, 129, 133–34, 142–43, 146, 147; ideas for films, 124–25; International Experimental Film Congress and, 13, 126, 127; Millennium Film Workshop and, 21–22, 31, 121–22, 127, 128, 129, 134; modes of filmmaking and, 123, 126–27, 133–35; montage in, 8, 15, 20, 36–41, 48–49, 84–85, 106, 118; overviews of oeuvre, 2, 10–15, 17–19, 77–79, 116–17, 151–57; personal vulnerability in films, 131–33; politics of biography and, 1–2, 7–10; popular culture in films, 43–44, 70, 71, 81–83, 92, 130–31, 139; repetition in, 39–41; second-wave feminism and, 1, 9, 117 (*see also* second-wave feminism); subjective memories/counter memories and, 50–55, 143–44; teaching by SF, 22, 146–48; titles of films, 15–17; travel with films, 128–30; writing text, 125. *See also titles of specific films*

Frohnmayer, John, 142

From the Ground Up, 18–19, 124

Gakuen, Seiju, 65–66

gay liberation politics, 11, 35, 66

Barbara Mennel is the Rothman Chair and Director of the Center for the Humanities and the Public Sphere and a professor of film studies at the University of Florida. Mennel's books include *Women at Work in Twenty-first Century European Cinema* and *Queer Cinema: Schoolgirls, Vampires, and Gay Cowboys*.

Books in the series Contemporary
Film Directors

The University of Illinois Press
is a founding member of the
Association of University Presses.

University of Illinois Press
1325 South Oak Street
Champaign, IL 61820-6903
www.press.uillinois.edu